Scott, Clifford H.

Lester Frank Ward

DATE			

Twayne's United States Authors Series

Sylvia E. Bowman, *Editor*

INDIANA UNIVERSITY

Lester Frank Ward

TUSAS 275

Lester Frank Ward

LESTER FRANK WARD

By CLIFFORD H. SCOTT

Indiana University at Fort Wayne

TWAYNE PUBLISHERS

A DIVISION OF G. K. HALL & CO., BOSTON

Library of Congress Cataloging in Publication Data

Scott, Clifford H
  Lester Frank Ward.

  (Twayne's United States authors series ; TUSAS 275)
  Bibliography: pp. 183–89.
  Includes index.
  1. Ward, Lester Frank, 1841–1913.
HM22.U6W35   301'.092'4 [B]   76–16539
ISBN 0–8057–7175–1

Contents

About the Author

Clifford H. Scott, author of *Lester Frank Ward*, is chairman and associate professor of history at Indiana University–Purdue University at Fort Wayne. Professor Scott received his A.B. with highest honors from the University of Northern Iowa and his Ph.D. from the University of Iowa. Recipient of a Woodrow Wilson Fellowship, a University of Iowa Dissertation Fellowship, Indiana University Faculty Fellowships, and a National Science Foundation Fellowship, Scott has centered his research attention on the social application of ideas in science and the perception of ethnic differences in late nineteenth-century and early twentieth-century America.

Scott has read research papers on Protestant missionary perceptions of black Africans before the Organization of American Historians, the women's reform ideas of Lester Ward before the American Historical Association, and the images of black Africans in American fiction before the Popular Culture Association. Articles based on these papers have appeared in *The Historian* and in the *North Dakota Quarterly*. Scott has also contributed book reviews to the *Indiana Magazine of History* and to the *Journal of the West*. He is presently engaged in a community study to discover how World War I altered ethnic ideas and assimilation patterns in a heavily German-American urban area.

Besides his classroom and research work, Scott is actively engaged in the American Association of University Professors, having recently served as president of the Indiana Conference of that professional faculty organization.

Preface

By no inflation of literary rubric can Lester Frank Ward be viewed as a major American writer. He did not possess the craftsmanship of Henry James, the sustained logic of Charles S. Peirce, or the esthetic sensitivities of Henry Adams. Nor do his extensive paleobotanical studies and numerous sociological works carry great importance in contemporary natural science and social science. Rather, Ward's intellectual significance and the justification for this study lie in his efforts to reconcile mid-nineteenth-century democratic assumptions and ideas with late-nineteenth-century, radical intellectual and value changes resulting from scientific work in biology and from the urban-industrial transformation of American life. That intellectual and social revolution which Ward and other observers perceived in their day is not only still with us; it currently threatens to overwhelm us. How Ward attempted to understand and cope with an intellectual and social environment in rapid transformation provides us with a perspective to better understand his era, its intellectual and literary spokesmen, and, ultimately, ourselves.

Ward championed a belief in the potential of "common men," a faith inspired by his own background and experience. Universal public education, operating within a framework of democratic national government, could release, he contended, the human talent necessary to exploit scientific knowledge for humanistic ends. Thereby, Ward believed, it would be possible for Americans to maintain the essence of their historical values within a world of evolutionary physical and social change. Man was not the pawn of deterministic natural forces, as many scientists, social philosophers, and writers had begun to conclude; for man held the intellectual power to direct those forces in an evolutionary direction of his own choice.

In this book I first explore Ward's life to establish a framework for the subsequent description and analysis of his ideas; and I then examine in successive chapters his major intellectual concerns in the areas of education, science, government, sociology, and religion. These subjects were intimately related in Ward's mind, and he proceeded in a half dozen volumes and scores of articles to explain that relationship and its meaning to man. These writings—with the exception of his purely paleobotanical monographs which I have omitted—his correspondence, and his personal papers provide the major sources of this study.

I would like to acknowledge my special appreciation to the library staffs of the John Hay Memorial Library at Brown University and the Indiana University at Fort Wayne Library, the material assistance of Indiana University Summer Fellowships and Grants-in-Aid, the National Science Foundation, and the editorial supervision of Professor Sylvia Bowman.

CLIFFORD H. SCOTT

Indiana University at Fort Wayne

Chronology

1841   Lester Frank Ward born June 18 in Joliet, Illinois; tenth and youngest child of Justus—an itinerant millwright—and Silence Ward.

1842–   Family moves about to new mill sites in central Illinois.
1852

1855   Family moves to land bounty claim in Buchanan County, Iowa.

1857   Father dies; Ward returns to Illinois to attend school and work as an agricultural laborer. First short stories.

1858   Moves to home of older brother, Cyrenus Osborn Ward, in Pennsylvania.

1861   Attends three terms of the Susquehanna Collegiate Institute, Towanda, Pennsylvania (1861–1862).

1862   August 13, marries Lizzie Caroline Vought; August 26, mustered into the Pennsylvania Volunteers.

1863   Wounded three times at the Battle of Chancellorsville on May 3.

1864   Discharged November 18 from the Veterans Reserve Corps.

1865   Hired by the Treasury Department, Washington, D. C., as a minor clerk. Birth of Ward's only child, Roy Fontaine, who died in infancy.

1867   Transferred and promoted to the Bureau of Statistics. Enrolls in night classes at Columbian College (George Washington University).

1869   Begins a proposed book, "The Great Panacea." Bachelor of Arts from Columbian College.

1870   Made chief of the Division of Navigation and Immigration in the Bureau of Statistics. Editor of *The Iconoclast*, a rationalist paper of the National Liberal Reform League (March 1870–September 1871).

1871   Bachelor of Laws from Columbian College; admitted to the bar.

1872   First wife, Lizzie Caroline, dies March 25. Begins first botanical excursions. Granted Master of Arts from Columbian College.

1873   Second marriage to Rosamond Simons Pierce, a widow, March 6.

1875   Five months on assignment as a botanist on one of the John Wesley Powell surveys in Utah Territory. Publication of articles in various scientific periodicals.

1877   Botanical excursion to Texas with the American Association for the Advancement of Science. Regular attendance at national scientific meetings.

1878   Founding member of the Cosmos Club; member of the Philosophical Society of Washington, D. C., the Biological Society, and the Anthropological Society.

1881   Resigns from the Bureau of Statistics to join John Wesley Powell's Geological Survey as chief of the Division of Fossil Plants and honorary curator of botany and fossil plants of the National Museum.

1880's   Yearly field trips to the Rockies, the West Coast, and the Atlantic Coast.

1882   *Guide to the Flora of Washington, D. C. and Vicinity.*

1883   Publication of *Dynamic Sociology* in two volumes.

1884   Taught night school as professor of botany for the Corcoran Scientific School, Columbian College, 1884–1886.

1887   *Synopsis of the Flora of the Laramie Group* and *Geographical Distribution of Fossil Plants.*

1889   *Geographical Distribution of Fossil Plants* and *The Cretaceous Formation of the Black Hills as indicated by the Fossil Plants.*

1890's   Field work in the Black Hills, the Rocky Mountains, the West Coast, and Atlantic coastal areas; minor publications. Part time and summer lectures in botany and in sociology at various chautauquas and universities.

1892   Promoted to chief paleontologist in the Geological Survey. Vice-president of the Section on Economic Science and Statistics of the American Association for the Advancement of Science.

Chronology

1893 *The Psychic Factors of Civilization.*

1894 *The Potomac Formation.* Attends the International Geological Congress in Zurich.

1896 Advisory editor of the fledgling *American Journal of Sociology. Some Analogies in the Lower Cretaceous of Europe and America.*

1897 Doctor of Laws from Columbian College.

1898 *Outlines of Sociology.*

1899 *The Cretaceous Formation of the Black Hills.* Botany entries in *Webster's International Dictionary,* 1899–1900.

1900 Summer in London and Paris. Elected president of the Institut International de Sociologie for 1900–1903. *Status of the Mesozoic Floras of the United States* (part one).

1903 *Pure Sociology.* Summer in Europe; visits Ludwig Gumplowicz. Botany entries in the *Century Dictionary,* 1903–1906.

1904 *Status of the Mesozoic Floras of the United States* (part two).

1905 Resigns from the Geological Survey. *A Text-Book of Sociology,* co-authored with James Quayle Dealey of Brown University.

1906 *Applied Sociology.* Summer in Europe. Professor of Sociology at Brown University. President of the American Sociology Society.

1909 Summer in Europe at the Berne Congress of the International Institut de Sociologie.

1910– Summer lectures at the University of Wisconsin and at
1911 Columbia University. To Europe for the Monist Congress at Hamburg; visits Ernst H. Haeckel, a naturalist and creator of theory of materialistic monism.

1913 Dies April 18, Washington, D. C., while visiting his invalid wife.

1913– *Glimpses of the Cosmos,* in six volumes; a collection of
1918 Ward's lesser published writings with autobiographical comment.

CHAPTER 1

The Life of Lester Frank Ward

I A Son of the Middle Border

LESTER Ward seldom mentioned his family or early background. "Pride of ancestry is a mark of degeneracy," he claimed in late life; and he insisted that his mind had been "trimmed to the future rather than the past."[1] Such hard-minded braggadocio more clearly suggests that Ward spent much of his life attempting to escape his origins by moving into new fields of science where social background and established education had only marginal significance. For Ward's family were among the plain people of the early nineteenth century: evangelical Protestant, hard-working, foot-loose, and not very successful by most standards. His father, Justus Ward, had been born in New Hampshire in the 1780's; had moved to New York State, where he had married right after the War of 1812; and had then attempted to earn a living as a farmer, mechanic, and construction worker. His bride of 1816 was Silence Loomis Rolph, a New Yorker, whose father was a minister with literary interests that had led him to translate Homer's *Iliad*. While Lester's father was apparently a stern and work-oriented man, his mother, according to his later recollections, was "scholarly, refined and fond of literary pursuits, of high attainments, with versatility of gifts and accomplishments."[2] Her few preserved letters confirm Ward's view, but he purposely avoided mentioning that she was also strongly religious and that she encouraged her sons to enter the ministry.

In New York, the Wards had eight children. In the mid-1830's, the elder Ward was attracted to Illinois to build locks on the Illinois and Michigan Canal that was being constructed between Lake Michigan and LaSalle, Illinois. Settling in Joliet,

13

a small canal town, the Wards had another son, Erastus, in 1838, and then, on June 18, 1841, when his father was fifty-four and his mother forty-five, Lester Frank was born. Justus had a strong entrepreneurial spirit for he soon purchased a quarry to supply stones for the canal locks; and a year later he moved from Joliet to erect a sawmill near the village of Cass in order to build a towpath across the Des Plaines swamps. In 1850, the family moved once again, to St. Charles, Illinois, and two years later to a farm and sawmill on a tributary of the Fox River near St. Charles.

While the father and an older brother struggled to tame nature for man's use and to direct her power for their own gain, Lester and Erastus had time to indulge their curiosity by roving through the woods and meadows of the Fox River valley. The responsibility of earning a livelihood was, however, constantly brought to the boys' attention; and the young entrepreneurs gathered nuts for sale, hunted birds and small game and also held part time jobs at the mill and in St. Charles. Their early schooling derived directly from nature and from the strong Protestant ethic of work and frugality presented by their parents' daily lives, but some formal education was found during the winter months at a rural school near Cass and during the 1850's in St. Charles.

With the partial completion of the canal and with the introduction of the railroad to Illinois, Justus Ward was forced to shift stride in his mobile pursuit of a living. Since he had been reared on a farm, he took advantage of a change in the military land bounty law of 1850 to apply for a land grant based on his brief War of 1812 military record. Considerable difficulty confronted Ward in clearing his claim; but, even before it had been authorized, he looked westward to establish a new homestead. The mill near St. Charles was sold to an older son, and the Ward family in the spring of 1855 set out by covered wagon through Galena and Dubuque for the one hundred and sixty acres Justus claimed in Buchanan County, Iowa. During the trip, which took nearly all summer, Lester and Erastus hunted waterfowl and small game for food during the day and slept under the wagon at night. According to Lester, the trip was "one of the most memorable, as well as most enjoyable events of my early life."[3] Justus and Silence Ward were met in Iowa by their eldest son, Lorenzo Rolph Ward, and his family. In the rolling open prairie of eastern Iowa, the boys developed an intense love of nature that contributed later to Lester's becoming a naturalist. Years later he recalled how he had enjoyed wandering among the prairie wildflowers, although he had had no knowledge of their names or about how they might be studied systematically. Worse yet for the boy's educational ambitions, there were no schools nearby.

The family had been in Iowa only a year and a half when the seventy-year-old Justus died in January 1857. When Mrs. Ward decided to return to the more settled area of St. Charles to live with her only daughter, Erastus and Lester Frank elected to return to Illinois with their mother for they were confident that they could hire themselves to former neighbors and also take advantage of the greater schooling that St. Charles offered. After their return, the boys boarded out during the Illinois crop season of 1857 doing farm chores and harvesting corn and wheat. During the winter, they moved into St. Charles to keep "bachelor's house" in the abandoned frame home used by their family six years before and to attend grammar school. Ward recalled later that, while they had less than enough to eat, they had read voraciously during those winter months. Schoolbooks, French and Latin readers, local newspapers and the New York *Ledger*, and as many ten cent novels as they could buy or barter comprised the boys' reading material. During the winter, Ward began a lifelong habit of keeping a diary written in French to assist his language training.

Lester's attraction to the exciting romances of the novels and newspaper serials led him to write his own short stories, several of which were published in the St. Charles *Argus*. "The Spaniard's Revenge," the only story which survives, reveals that many of Ward's social attitudes were already formed.[4] The story of a Spanish lad's unsuccessful efforts to free his lover from a convent derides the interference of parents with their children's lives, places a high value on gaining respect, and severely attacks the Catholic Church for its use of force in maintaining a prison-like atmosphere in nunneries. After telling his tale of blood, unrequited love, and Catholic villainy, the sixteen-year-old adventure writer found no other solution for his protagonist except a melodramatic suicide. Fortunately, Ward never again attempted fiction.

As the winter of 1857–1858 passed with the Ward boys alone in the drafty house in St. Charles, they dreamed high dreams of Western adventure, language accomplishments, economic and social success, beautiful Spanish ladies, and the destruction of the Catholic Church's power. In the spring, Lester and Erastus received word that still another brother, Cyrenus Osborn Ward, needed help in his small wagon-hub factory in Myersburg, Pennsylvania. Twenty-year-old Erastus and seventeen-year-old Lester, excited with hopes of economic gain and about the superior education available in the Myersburg-Towanda area, travelled afoot, while working their way from a "backward region" to a "more enlightened one."[5]

II Coming of Age

Northeastern Pennsylvania, unfortunately, was not yet the Promised Land. While it did bring companionship and social entertainment for the boys with other youths their age, it did not produce the economic or educational rewards they had dreamed about. The recession of 1858 kept the ill-financed wagon-hub shop from increasing its sales, and it continued into decline. In 1860, Lester, taking his back pay in wagon hubs that he periodically bartered during his remaining two years in Pennsylvania, left the failing shop to seek agricultural labor in the area. Ward's diary, after he had left the wagon-hub shop, contains a faithful record of the constant economic problems of an itinerant laborer not yet at his majority.[6] An intricate system of barter and loans kept him afloat, but Ward dreamed with deep longing of obtaining a formal education, of marrying a sweetheart he had acquired in Myersburg, and of becoming a wealthy, respected professional man.

His torrid courtship of Lizzie (Elizabeth Caroline) Vought, a poor shoemaker's daughter, revealed Ward's incurable romanticism, exuberant ego, and the sexual mores of the rural working class. More than the meals dispensed by her family, the intimate affections of Lizzie sustained Lester during these years. Without money, Ward did have dreams. In July 1861, he wrote in his diary that, if he could only borrow one hundred and seventy-five dollars, "what a fine world this would be then! ... She [Lizzie] could obtain an education, and I could soon establish myself in some business which would earn me enough to put me through college and her also, and I could study law and set up an office, and then I could marry her, my sweet girl, and what a sweet life. But that is all air-castles."[7]

Politics in 1860 and 1861 provided alternative satisfactions as the young Ward, following the Whiggish habits of his father and the strong idealism of his mother, quickly identified with the Abolitionist wing of the Republican party against the wealthy slaveowners who forced slaves to work without economic hope or education and who blessed the custom in the name of religion. Political debates were a principal entertainment in Bradford County, along with attending church services; and Ward played an active part in both.

In 1860, Lester was able to find a job teaching in a township school for six dollars a month with boarding rights. This work brought in enough money, with the addition of loans from various friends and relatives, for him to attend the Susquehanna Collegiate Institute at nearby Towanda, Pennsylvania, for two terms in 1861 and for one in 1862. After sufficient preparation at the institute, Ward hoped to enter Lafayette College at Easton to study law. Ward enjoyed these student days, furiously studying, writing essays, playing football, and courting his girl. Yet his undercurrent of fear that he might not be able to attend college, which would be much more expensive and socially difficult than the institute, runs throughout his diary. The hunger for respectability was a powerful hunger; Ward knew that even in Towanda the socially and economically better off youth could not or would not fully accept him into their ranks. The result was an outwardly shy and nonaggressive youth who found it "a difficult thing to conquer an inborn feeling of self-depreciation."[8]

Ward channelled his desire for both Lizzie and social standing into his studies. His essays of the period reflected his position: "Mental Application," "The Utility of a Debating Society," "Self-Made Men," "Aspiration," "The Influence of Education on Our

Nation," and "Liberty for the Negroes." Debate was his real forte, however, and he entered each topic in his diary: "That Negroes Have More Cause for Complaint Than the Indians," "That Women Have More Influence Over Men Than Money," "That Women Should Learn and Practice the Art of Public Speaking," "That the Masses Are More Important to Maintain the Nation Than the Rulers," and "That Slavery is a Greater Harm Than Intemperance."

After one night's debate over whether parents were under more obligation to their children than the children were to their parents, Ward tellingly wrote, "I had the aff[irmative] and won. Glorious victory!"[9] Ward had left his elderly mother behind with some regret, but not with enough to motivate a return to visit her—although she lived until nearly 1880—or to exchange letters with her on more than a yearly basis. Ward did not feel he owed his parents anything, but the thought left him uneasy. In an essay of 1892, "The Reciprocal Obligations of Parents and Children," he argued that, after the age of dependence, the account was settled between parents and child.[10]

Since children were seldom conceived by rational choice but rather by sensual desire, he wrote, parents had only a limited claim to their children's devotion. Custom and common law, on the contrary, required a child to labor years for his parents with no legal obligation on their part to insure that he had been provided an adequate education. The relationship was little different, therefore, from the one between master and slave; many a young person, he wrote, had an unuttered feeling that something was wrong with such a system. Parents claimed the respect and labor of their children, but they accepted no responsibility for their shortcomings. In an autobiographical comment, Ward added, "I have known a boy who, when whipped by his father and told he was 'a good-for-nothing plague and did not earn his salt,' would hiss back into the teeth of his irate parent: 'you made me so.'"[11]

Ward's tumultuous romance with Lizzie Vought paralleled the course of the nation during 1861 and 1862 as the Civil War and his romance were waged warmly. By the spring and summer of 1862, some of his friends were volunteering for the Union, as had his closest brother, Erastus. Having taken almost everything that the Collegiate Institute could offer, Ward was still without funds for college. Working in the fields that summer, vocationally thwarted but emotionally and publicly committed to both Lincoln and Lizzie, he reached a logical decision: he would unite with both. On August 12, the handsome six foot Ward, responding to Lincoln's call for volunteers, enlisted in Myersburg as a private in the 141st Regiment of the Pennsylvania Volunteers. The next day he and Lizzie were married in Myersburg without friends or relatives present. Since the twenty-five dollar bounty paid Ward for volunteering was inadequate to support a family, he borrowed a wagon the following day and drove about selling some of the wagon hubs still in his possession. The short honeymoon, such as it was, ended quickly; Ward had to leave in five days for Harrisburg.

III   A *Soldier's Life*

On the afternoon of May 3, 1863, the still untried rural Pennsylvania troops of the Third Corps were on General Joe Wheeler's left flank as he confronted Robert E. Lee at Chancellorsville, Virginia. When Lee sent Stonewall Jackson's force against the exposed flank, Private Lester Ward found his idealism sorely tested. As he later wrote home to a Bradford County newspaper, with more bravado than he must have felt in his hospital bed, "I was chuckling over this grand opportunity offered me for thinning out the enemies of human liberty when a silent messenger came...."[12] Not one but three silent messengers ended Ward's ideological revelry by slamming into his thighs and his right knee. Ward was held captive by the Rebels for nearly two weeks before being exchanged for Confederate wounded. A lieutenant colonel who was wounded and captured with Ward wrote a few months later that Ward had "behaved with great gallantry" in the field. Young Ward's more personal judgment of the war was revealed years later when he told a confidant of the death of a young flag carrier next to him at Chancellorsville: "It was so pitiful, so useless, so ugly, I stopped and covered the lad with his beautiful flag."[13]

Ward spent the summer of 1863 in the Union hospital at Fairfax Seminary, Virginia, and on medical furlough in Pennsyl-

vania. On his return in the fall to Fairfax, following his Pennsylvania convalescence, he was transferred to the Veteran's
Reserves Corps which nominally guarded the capitol and as-
sisted in handling army supplies. Utilizing his time well, Ward
tutored officers in French and Latin and was soon promoted
to sergeant. Characteristic of his feelings at the time was a
personal slight suffered one day while tutoring a military and
social superior in Latin. The captain in question recited his
lesson well enough, but he made no effort to introduce Ward
to a girl waiting in his room. Wrote the angered Ward later in
the evening, "It was not that I had any desire to make her
acquaintance, but I wish to be treated as a gentleman."[14] There
was more than one kind of battlefield for a proud and ambitious
young man.

While the army was no place to expect treatment as a gentleman, a good deal of laxity was allowed the enlisted men in their
quartering. Ward sent for Lizzie, and the two established housekeeping. Ever the entrepreneur, Ward bought some utensils
and began taking orders for fresh pies which he and Lizzie
baked for the troops. The two also did laundry for the men,
and they reported in one month's time a profit of over a hundred
dollars. Weekends, the couple hitched rides into Washington,
tramped the corridors of the capitol, watched the animals feed-
ing near the uncompleted Washington Monument, and examined
the exhibits at the Smithsonian Institution.

By the fall of 1864, their life, while not too uncomfortable and
more affluent than either had ever known, became "static"—
Ward's favorite phrase. Lizzie was pregnant, and Ward had
little future in the Invalid Reserve Corps. Ward applied for a
disability discharge, and he left the army on November 18, 1864.
After a short trip back home to Pennsylvania to be commended
by the townfolk, to engage in several debates in the now
parochial Collegiate Institute, and to deposit his pregnant Lizzie
with her parents, Ward returned to Washington to collect what
the government owed him—a job.

IV   A Washington Education

While in the Veteran's Reserve, various officers had assured
Ward that, with his military record, education, and drive, it

would be easy to obtain a clerkship. They were wrong. Securing a government position was painfully difficult, and Ward began to receive a considerable education in the ways of Washington during the lean winter and spring months of 1865. Wounded veterans applying for jobs formed long lines at the offices of the departmental secretaries. Without intercession from other government officials, the men had no possibility of employment. Ward carefully rationed his mustering-out pay as he moved downward in roominghouses each month and consoled himself by reading Virgil in the Latin.

Persistence was Ward's watchword in the spring of 1865; he sent countless letters to the Pensions Bureau, the Secretary of the Treasury, the Secretary of War, congressional representatives from Illinois and Pennsylvania; and, he finally, in mounting desperation, wrote to President Lincoln. Temporary work in the Claims Office in February gave Ward hope and twenty dollars, which he immediately spent for a new suit, "a superb garment of mixed silk."[15] But in April double tragedy struck Ward: the deaths of Lincoln, whom he revered, and of his brother Erastus. Erastus's death from battlefield wounds drove Ward into deep sorrow over the loss of "this Christian, this Martyr."[16] Fortunately for Ward's morale at this low point in early May, the Treasury Department—due either to his persistence, to Congressman John Farnsworth of Illinois, or to Ward's new silk suit—notified him that a temporary clerkship would become permanent for him in July. While examining the quartermaster's accounts in the third auditor's office was hardly "dynamic," especially for one who had always disliked mathematics, the job did allow Ward to send for Lizzie, rent a house, and immediately plunge into debt.

On June 14, 1865, a son was born to the Wards and was named Roy Fontaine. Ward had mentioned Lizzie's pregnancy only once in his diary prior to the boy's birth, but several references during their stay at the Fairfax army base referred to birth control measures. Apparently Ward was not enthusiastic about becoming a parent before he had saved enough money to attend college and become a lawyer; for he had retained his occupational dream. But the baby, always sickly, contracted pneumonia; and in May 1866 the child "went to Heaven, where

he will live forever the life of endless joy."[17] For the surviving
parents, too much had to be done to permit prolonged mourning.

Postwar Washington was filled with ambition; and, since a
first class clerkship was the lowest step in the government hier-
archy, there was nowhere to go but upward. Ward, who found
it simple to accomplish his auditing tasks in less than the nine
to three o'clock hours of the Treasury Department, filled his
idle time reading and writing essays. He soon joined the temperance society to which his division chief belonged and maneuvered
to form acquaintances who could introduce him into local debating societies. In one of the latter, the Concordia Lyceum,
he became an officer and an enthusiastic debater. There was
an abundance of debate and intrigue in Washington from 1865
to 1868. Ward and Lizzie went over to the congressional cham-
bers several times a week and stayed late at night to watch
the debates about Reconstruction policy. Ward closely identified
with "radical" Representatives William Kelly and Thaddeus
Stevens from Pennsylvania and with Senator Charles Sumner
of Massachusetts. Because of Ward's fervor, he joined the
Suffrage League, a dangerous thing for him to do since treasury
employees were being fired for speech and actions that were
not loyal to President Johnson's policy.

At home, Ward attempted to amass the possessions that would
reassure him that he was succeeding in life. New silk suits
and top hats, a new watch, a six hundred dollar Chickering
piano, a new violin, carpets, and furniture quickly depleted his
one hundred and fifty dollar a month salary. On December 24,
1865, for example, Ward borrowed fifty dollars on his month's
wages, spent forty-four on clothing for himself, six for his wife,
and charged a chicken at the market for Christmas dinner. A
delicate and refined system of loans and cross-loans fill Ward's
check stubs for the period; and, because of the high cost of
his subsidizing *Dynamic Sociology* in 1883, debt was to be the
story of his financial life until about 1890.

Ward and Lizzie both played the piano, and Ward played
the violin as well. They read to each other in the evening: Victor
Hugo in French, Herodotus in Greek, Charles Dickens, and the
Bible. Diverse speakers and performers appeared in Washington,
and the Wards enjoyed hearing temperance speeches, women's

rights advocates, capital punishment reformers, and other orators throughout the week. In addition, Lizzie attended women's seminaries and tutored in French and Latin, as did Lester. In 1868, they built a new home large enough to accommodate male roomers from among Ward's friends at the office.

At work, Ward managed to be invited to help staff the new Bureau of Statistics established within the Treasury Department in January 1867. Within a year, he was promoted a grade; and, within three years, he was made chief of the small division concerned with navigation and immigration statistics. This position was less routine than checking accounts, and Ward wrote in his diary that for the first time he really enjoyed his duties. In 1869, Ward again petitioned for promotion on the grounds of his loyalty to Grant and his past opposition to ex-President Johnson's repudiated policies. With the aid of a partisan letter from Representative Ulysses Mercur of Pennsylvania, he advanced to a grade three clerkship. By 1871, with strong letters from his bureau chief in his behalf, along with additional political encouragement, Ward finally gained a grade four appointment; but none of his efforts was ever successful in attempting to become a bureau chief. In 1872, he assumed the duties of librarian of the Bureau of Statistics and remained in that post until he transferred to the Geological Survey in 1881.

In 1869, Ward wrote an unpublished essay on "Washington City" that provides a glimpse of how he viewed his bureaucratic position in the capitol.[18] The lowest class in the city, he held, were the government clerks, a subordinate race with no rights that anyone else had to respect. After a month of driving a quill, all that they received was paid by them to the Jews and hucksters. Taking government service, he complained, was comparable to taking the black veil of the Saint Bernard nuns; for, having entered such service, one could not escape. The only escape was to rise upward; for, when one had crossed to the two thousand dollar a year salary, he became an "officer" who could prey upon his subordinates for annual gifts; however, one had to have much tact and influence to reach that rank:

Great talents, superior skill or depth of learning enter not into this qualification. He [who would advance] must possess an interested

friend whose name stands high upon the scroll of fame to make
intercession for him. But most of all he must support the administration, right or wrong. He must be prepared and willing to wink
at corruption, praise those in power, excuse official perjury and
bow obsequious to usurpation. He must not scruple to compel his
convictions of right to take all convenient shades of color, and if
necessary undergo sudden and complete inversions to suit the occasion. In short these positions are given in exchange for the soul.[19]

Ward preferred the educational ladder. A block payment of
one hundred and fifty dollars in the spring of 1867 to all clerks
gave him sufficient capital to pay most of his debts and to make
a down payment on returning to the formal education of his
dreams. Like Henry Adams, only at a much lower social class
level, Ward was unsure about how to obtain an education or
about what vocation was best suited for his talents in Washington. When he visited professors at Columbian College (after
the turn of the century, George Washington University), he
convinced them of the utility of offering special night classes
for government clerks. By 1869, Ward had raced through the
Columbian curricula to gain his Bachelor of Arts degree, while
Lizzie at the same time received her valedictory certificate
from Women's Union Seminary.

Since a Bachelor of Arts diploma did not satisfy Ward, he
returned to night school in the fall to achieve his deferred
ambition of becoming a lawyer. A Bachelor of Laws was awarded
to him in the spring of 1871 along with admission to the local
bar association; but for reasons not totally clear, Ward never
attempted to practice. Years later he joked that his conscience
would not allow him to practice either law or medicine; but it
is more likely that without either capital or a practice, Ward
found it impossible in lawyer-packed Washington to obtain the
professional independence that he had once believed a law
degree could produce. As a result, he completed his Master of
Arts degree in 1872 with an emphasis in science that also
certified him to practice medicine.

On the basis of his hard-won degrees, Ward requested that
the director of the Bureau of Statistics rescue him from the
mechanical work assigned him and give him something suitable
for his education. Furthermore, Ward complained, the bureau's

chief clerk had told him to go "suck his thumbs" if he did not have enough to do.[20] To appease his drive for more fulfilling employment, Ward began work at home and at the office on a proposed book, "The Great Panacea," a scientific paean to education that paralleled his course of study at Columbian College. Ward never regretted the hours and the paper that he had borrowed from his official work in order to pursue this private study: "From 1865 to 1881, I must insist that the only really useful work I ever did, work that counts in any way for the general good of my race—dynamic work—was wholly unofficial. I have often thought that sinecure positions... are among the great agencies of human progress."[21]

Ward's work on his never-ending manuscript was interrupted during 1870 and 1871 when he and a group of government clerks organized a National Liberal Reform League with Ward as editor of their monthly paper, *The Iconoclast*. The anticleric and skeptical paper absorbed all of Ward's free time in his efforts to increase its circulation, to write many of its articles and editorials, and to secure adequate financing. Unhappily for the editor, this open attack on religious and secular superstition and on institutional oppressions of various sorts won few converts. Ward reflected in later life that frontal assaults like those at Chancellorsville and in *The Iconoclast* were not such effective agents for reform as the slower but more steady undermining of false public ideas and assumptions by more conventional writing and teaching. The lesson remained with Ward for a lifetime.

In March 1872, while Ward was working nights in the laboratories of Columbian College to complete his Master of Arts, Lizzie had an attack of appendicitis; and, before Lester knew what had happened, he had become a widower. There had been a powerful emotional tie between him and Lizzie which under his encouragement had led to a deepening intellectual companionship between the two. He had been improving not only himself but also his wife who had shared his impoverished origins. Lizzie's death sank Ward in deep melancholy. As he wrote subsequently in the third person of one who had become separated from himself, "This sad event threw a gloom over his life and left a blank never again completely filled...."[22]

To combat his depression, Ward in April started taking long

walks on the outskirts of Washington, in the parks, and along the undeveloped Rock Creek area into Woodley Park. While he was attempting to regain the joy in living that he had known as a boy who roamed the wilds, his mind was attracted by his biology studies at Columbian and by how he might profitably bring together both his education and his emotional recuperation. As a result, he threw himself into the collection of botanical and zoological specimens and increased his readings in the rapidly advancing biological sciences.

His recovery was quickened even more by a chance meeting with a widow from New York, Rose Simons Pierce, who had moved to Washington to be with her father, who worked for the post office, and with her older sisters who were married to government clerks. In the late spring or early summer of 1872, Ward penned a remarkable letter to the young widow. "I scarcely know you at all," he conceded in his virtual marriage proposal; but he wished to know whether she would take offense if he began to pay her court so soon after the death of his wife. Not waiting for a response or hiding his own romantic feelings, he confessed that "I am only happy when you are present in person or in thought, and a fluttering sensation of joy over which I have no control takes possession of me every time I come into your presence."[23] The outcome of such emotion was never in doubt, for Rose's cousin married them March 6, 1873.

Ward continued his biological excursions, but he now was accompanied by his father-in-law, Frank Simons, and by his brother-in-law, John Comstock. For nearly two years he collected birds, pickled rodents and assorted reptiles, and worked on his education manuscript. Rose pasted his plant specimens in large notebooks, handled the labeling chores, did most of the copying of material for local flora catalogues and guides; and she enjoyed not only such intellectual activity but also the promotion of her husband's reputation. It was she who cared for Lester Frank's proud scrapbook collection of personal memorabilia that by the end of his life numbered twenty-three volumes. In 1873 and 1874, Ward and Rose, with her money and his loans, built a large home at 1466 Rhode Island Avenue with room set aside for an herbarium and science workshop.

Shortly before construction began in 1873, Ward had joined the Potomac-Side Naturalist Club, a local society composed of government scientists in the Department of Agriculture and the Smithsonian Institution, science professors at Columbian and other nearby schools, and a few medical doctors. At the naturalist club, Ward delivered papers based on his nature jaunts and published brief articles on the local flora. At the club Ward met and was captivated by the Washington scientific lion, Major John Wesley Powell. Powell, the hero of the private exploration of the Lower Colorado River in 1869, was in Washington securing funds and the authorization of the Department of Interior for additional exploration of the Lower Colorado River territory. Ward and Powell had much in common: both were from Illinois, having come of age amid a nature that excited their curiosity; both had strongly evangelical parents whose values they were now secularizing and restructuring into a scientific framework; both were idealistic Union soldiers who had suffered for their service (Powell had lost most of his right arm at Shiloh); and now both looked to the progressive development of the national government for their future.

In the spring of 1875, Major Powell secured a summer transfer for Ward to serve as botanist for his fourth expedition to the Wasatch Mountains region of Utah and as a collector of specimens for the government's scientific display planned for the 1876 Philadelphia Centennial Exposition. A new world opened up for Ward during the five month expedition; he found that it was possible to earn a living and a reputation at the same time as he did what he most liked to do. When Ward returned home in the fall, he was inspired to obtain a scientific career; he worked furiously on his collection all winter; and he decided to recast his whole book in the scientific direction suggested by his now systematic reading of Augustus Comte, Herbert Spencer, Charles Lyell, John William Draper, Francis Bacon, and Ernst Haeckel. Each new idea discovered in his reading was carefully and methodically recorded by Ward in alphabetical order with full bibliographic citation in an "Index Rerum" so that he might have ready access to such ideas in his future writing. In the spring of 1876, he acquired additional experience in scientific classification by assisting Spencer Baird of the Smithsonian in assembling the flora exhibits in Philadelphia.

But the various national surveys were under fire, and Powell in his efforts to unite them in one civilian agency was temporarily unable to mount any new expeditions. No new job was yet in sight for Ward. In fact, he had to move quickly to save his Bureau of Statistics sinecure during a budget paring of the sort that haunted government workers throughout Ward's career. To save his position, Ward requested that letters in his behalf be sent to the director by Congressmen Stephen Hurlbut and John Logan of Illinois, by Senator Richard Oglesby of Illinois, and by Major Powell; he also submitted an eight page legal-sized letter that outlined all he had accomplished for the bureau without the aid, he wrote, of outside political support![24] Since his position was preserved, Ward bided his time, working with the self-discipline that marked his life to gain a new Darwinian education, to embody his new learning in his revised manuscript, and to gain notice in the flurry of scientific societies being established in Washington. George Eliot's phrase, "A life apart from circumstantial things," became his ruling axiom as he disciplined himself to produce outside his immediate vocational environment.[25]

With Major Powell running interference, Ward in the late 1870's became a founding member of the Washington Biology Society, of which he became president in 1890 and 1891; of the Washington Anthropological Society; of the more exclusive Philosophical Society; and he also became founder of the gentlemen's social club—the Cosmos Club—that served to tie members of the various Washington societies into a common fraternity.

V   The 1880's: A Decade of Fulfillment

By 1879, Ward's manuscript was completely revised and re-titled "Dynamic Sociology" because of the influence of Comte. But the difference between a manuscript and a book is a publisher, and Ward did not have one. He had been able to publish only one brief extract in a science periodical, and all the publishers he contacted were unwilling to gamble with two volumes of erudite philosophical-scientific speculations that were offensive to both orthodox religious publishers and readers. Going to Major Powell with his problem, Ward found new support with letters from Powell to several New York editors including Edward L. Youmans, whose *Popular Science Monthly* had been the advance agent for Herbert Spencer in America. Youmans managed to secure an agreement for publication of the manuscript from the Appleton Company, but only on the condition that Ward provide nearly twenty-three hundred dollars to guarantee publishing costs. Finally, with the cooperation of Rose who had been giving substantial help to her husband by recopying his manuscript drafts, Ward found a way: they agreed to sell their mortgaged home to Rose's sister, Sarah Comstock, who was recently widowed and who would move in with them while they paid rent to her. With the equity money this sale provided and with various loans from fellow government employees, Ward's money enabled Appleton to publish in 1883 the two volume labor of love that Ward had spent nearly fifteen years of early morning, late night, and weekend effort in completing.

Meanwhile, Major Powell gathered in the product of his earlier labors. A new unified Geological Survey was formed in 1880 in a compromise of departmental politics and scientific rivalries; the following year Powell was offered its directorship; and he immediately invited Ward and other young men of various talents in Washington to join this well-funded and ambitious scientific bureau. The forty-year-old Ward, after sixteen years of pushing a quill, had at last an authentic vocational choice of becoming either a geologist in the survey or a linguist in the Bureau of Ethnology which was also headed by Powell. "It was twenty years before I found my opportunity," Ward later recalled, "and then it was almost too late."[26]

Ward opted for the Geological Survey position although he knew precious little about either Indian languages or American geology; but, if nothing else, Ward was an experienced hand at picking up a new education; and Powell promised him full time to move into paleobotany, a new scientific discipline with less than a half dozen American researchers. The study of fossilized plants was only a few million years removed from the botanical studies with which Ward was familiar. Yet he hoped that such studies might have some utility to the Geological

Survey's announced task of mapping the national domain and of giving scientific assistance in a rational exploitation of the nation's mineral resources. To Ward, paleobotany promised a new field, uncrowded by men or theories, that was awaiting a new Darwin to explain in a synthetic theory the huge array of scientific facts in plant evolution that had been scarcely touched by Darwin or by his early followers.

Ward found the best decade of his life in the survey under Powell from 1881 until the director's forced resignation in 1893–1894. The change from the Bureau of Statistics, Ward wrote, was "intensely agreeable."[27] He now had his own office and a small staff in the main building of the Smithsonian, where he also served as honorary curator of fossil plants; and he was given nearly free reign in pursuing his studies. "Major Powell," Ward wrote, "was very liberal in his ideas of official duty.... With him it was all for science and the public good."[28] Moreover, Powell's objective of using scientists in the Geological Survey to map out for the public the most rational utilization of Western resources fit in precisely with Ward's own view of the role of government and of human intellect to control natural forces.

During summer field trips, Ward travelled extensively in national-domain territories and in states along the eastern seaboard. From July to October 1883, for example, Ward traversed the Yellowstone Park area and floated a thousand miles down the Missouri River from Fort Benton to Bismarck in a flatboat with paleontologist Charles A. White. During the remainder of each year, he endeavored to keep up with bibliography and related literature; and he labored to make sense out of his fossil collections in written reports and in scientific articles. At the same time, Ward maintained active memberships in Washington science and literary societies to which he regularly contributed papers. He built a library of paleobotanical works in the Smithsonian that was easily the best in the nation and possibly in the world, exchanged specimens with collectors around the globe, wheedled purchasing funds from Powell, and continued his classifying labors in the hope he could make a major theoretical innovation to evolutionary theory.

While most of Ward's energies during the 1880's were directed to the natural sciences—to paleobotany in the survey and to teaching botany from 1884 to and including 1886 for the Corcoran Scientific School of Columbian College—he never forgot his social reform and social philosophy concerns. In fact, he dropped his evening school botany professorship, as he explained in an 1887 letter to President James Welling of Columbian, because his pleasure in the biology field "threatened to absorb all those precious hours that I had consecrated to social science."[29] While he enjoyed the former, he admitted, he would be willing to put most of it behind him if he were offered a full time position in the social sciences in a first rate public university.

Between the time of his entry into the Geological Survey and his 1890 introduction by Richard Ely to Albion Small of Colby College—who was using Ward's *Dynamic Sociology* in his sociology courses—Ward penned twenty-one articles in the area he defined as sociology. Included in these articles was a severe review of William Graham Sumner's *What Social Classes Owe to Each Other*, but Ward's best popularized contribution was to his series for the *Forum*, a journal of opinion.[30] Most of these articles were based on lectures Ward delivered at various Washington societies, at the Smithsonian Saturday Lecture Series, at Unitarian meetings, and in nearby schools.

VI   *Increasing Sociology Interests*

In the 1890's, Ward spent even more of his off-duty hours and even some of his official ones reading and writing in social philosophy. Yet his official duties consumed a majority of his time since he was still making annual field trips to the Black Hills, the Pacific Northwest, California and Arizona, New England, and nearby Virginia and Maryland; he was also better able because of increased knowledge to tie together his vast paleobotanic evidence into comprehensive reports about the epoch periods of American vegetation. The huge monographs of distribution tables, plant figures, generalizations, and bibliography that Ward prepared for the survey's annual reports took a great deal of time and detailed labor. New hypotheses remained obscure, however, and the studies that earlier had seemed to take only a matter of years to complete, now promised to take a lifetime. And Ward, late to arrive in his mature vocation, was already in his fifties.

After Powell was forced out of the Geological Survey in 1894 because of Western congressional fear of his interference in their control of Western land distribution and because of Southern congressional criticism of the sums being spent in esoteric scientific research, Ward no longer found the survey so congenial. Because bureaucratic controls were introduced and because congressional pruning of funds—especially after the attack on Powell and the depression of 1893—forced numerous layoffs, Ward, physically separated from the survey in the Smithsonian Building, found his independence considerably lessened.

By matter of habit as well as of interest, Ward had joined the new rebel American Economic Association formed by Richard Ely of nearby Johns Hopkins University and other avant-garde economists. The association generally shared Ward's hostility to the Manchester School of laissez-faire economics, favored the application of scientific procedures to the study of the political economy, and believed governmental activity could improve the economy. Ward was well acquainted with Ely who belonged to the Cosmos Club and who frequently brought his graduate students to gaze in awe at Henry Adams, Alexander Graham Bell, Major Powell, Simon Newcomb, and other luminaries at the club. Ely's students were assigned to read *Dynamic Sociology,* and one, Edward Allsworth Ross—later a nationally prominent sociologist himself—sought out Ward for conversations; and, after becoming a friend of the family, he married Rose's niece and became Ward's nephew.

Ely wrote Ward in 1890 that Professor Albion Small, a minister converted to sociology, was using Ward's work in his Colby College classes. Ward wrote Small, and the two became close friends who encouraged each other in sociological pursuits. Sociology was just becoming a recognized academic subject, but considerable differences of opinion existed about what constituted its subject matter, methodology, and body of literature. The growth of the new field—one that reflected the increased social concerns of a socially uprooted society of industrialism, urbanism, and immigration—encouraged Ward to expand his sociological writing.

Moreover, interest in implementing the utopian world of Edward Bellamy's *Looking Backward*—"a sugar-coated bomb" Ward called the book—had led to the establishment of a Commonwealth Club in Washington. Ward's membership in the club and his acquaintance with Laurence Gronlund, a fellow member and a radical social critic, increased his interest in analyzing social action. Membership in another club, formed in 1889 to read the recent works of Arthur Schopenhauer, also prompted Ward to expand his earlier subjective treatment of the "philosophy of the feelings." Since *Dynamic Sociology* had sold very poorly, no more than five hundred copies in ten years, Ward hoped that a new book that more clearly explained his assurance that social reform was in harmony with science's understanding of nature would promote a friendlier reception for his ideas. Therefore, while collecting fossil specimens in Arizona during the summer of 1891, Ward gazed at the stars and drafted his chapter headings for a book detailing not only the psychological basis of sociology but also the dynamic possibilities of rational social control. Two years later, *The Psychic Factors of Civilization* was published, and Ward's reputation was increased in scientific circles as a sociologist and among sociologists as a scientist interested in their still ill-defined field.[31]

Shortly after Ward had initiated his friendship with the reform-minded Albion Small, the University of Chicago invited Small to establish a Department of Sociology at the new urban university and to become the editor of a sociology journal. Small moved quickly to create a department of bright young men, and he endeavored through his *American Journal of Sociology* to shape the development of the growing new social science. Anxious to add scientific respectability and the weight of a dignified author already in the general field, Small invited Ward to become an advisory editor of the journal and to contribute a series of articles that defined the relationship of sociology to other sciences. Ward, who had already written a series of twelve lectures for an extension course at The School of Sociology of Hartford, Connecticut, cooperated. Between the journal's first issue in 1896 and 1905, Ward was one of its most prolific con-

tributors in this effort to establish the legitimacy of both the
journal and the discipline. The initial series of Ward's articles
were incorporated into book form in 1898 and published as
Outlines of Sociology.[32]

VII *Many Roads to Follow*

By the turn of the century, Ward was fragmenting his efforts
even more than he had in earlier years. Since 1894, he had
averaged teaching one session of special sociology courses yearly
at places like The School of Sociology of Hartford, Connecticut,
the University of West Virginia, the University of Chicago, and
Stanford Junior College. In 1899, he had made a special investigation of the petrified forest region of western Arizona and had is-
sued a report recommending federal government preservation of
the area as a national monument. A colleague of Ward's at the
survey, Charles Walcott, introduced the Wards to the new
moneymaking diversion of writing the botanical entries for the
Supplement to *Webster's International Dictionary* and for the
Century Dictionary. The hourly wages were so superior to the
survey's two thousand dollars a year that Ward, Rose, and the
sister-in-law, Sarah Comstock, spent all their spare time in
dictionary work. By 1900, the survey shifted Ward to a per diem
salary to adjust for his time spent on lexicography, for his frequent trips to teach sociology, and for his visits to Europe for
other than geological reasons.

Ward's trips to Europe had become more frequent. In 1894,
he had attended the International Geological Congress at Zurich
as a representative of the survey since he was one of its few
members fluent in German and in the Romance languages and
since his policy of distributing several hundred gratis copies of
each of his various publications gave him a number of European
contacts. In 1900, he spent the summer in London and at the
Paris Congress of the newly organized Institut International de
Sociologie. The Institut, organized by European sociologists,
was held in conjunction with the Paris Exposition of 1900 and
invited prominent sociologists to deliver papers. Ward was
prominent—and also stately with his erect carriage, handsome
face, silver-grey hair and sidewhiskers, and his dignified French

delivery—and, to his genuine surprise, was elected president of the institut for its next meeting in 1903. During his 1903 summer on the Continent attending the International Geological Congress in Vienna and the Institut International de Sociologie, Ward paid a major visit to Graz, Austria, to visit Ludwig Gumplowicz, a social conflict theorist whose ideas Ward had introduced to American sociologists and who significantly influenced Ward's own thinking. In Paris, he was presented with France's highest academic award, the honorary degree of Officer of Public Education, in recognition of his work in the institut and his international advocacy of secular education.

Returned to America, Ward found himself increasingly disenchanted with his paleobotany work. Since the 1890's, the paleobotany study at the survey had been directed to the correlation of American geological formations with those of the Old World. The work went more slowly than Ward had anticipated, collections remained to be cleaned and classified, and the procedure was delicate and painstaking. As major difficulties developed in persuading the illustrations division of the survey to produce needed drawings and plates, Ward became increasingly cantankerous. When the survey was handed a fifty percent cut in funds in 1901 which required retrenchment in publications, Ward's verbosity, extended bibliographies, and expensive illustrations came under fire. Although his first paper on the Mesozoic floras appeared in 1900 and his second, finally, in 1904, Ward had become discouraged by the time the second paper appeared about ever completing the third, even though it had been begun. While preliminary investigations and collections had been made by him of some of the remaining formations, the physical work yet required in collections, in tedious classifying routines, in comparisons with the extant literature, and in the bureaucratic negotiations necessary to put together the monographs no longer whetted the sixty-three-year-old Ward's still sharp appetite for work:

If all had gone smoothly, I should have gone on and completed it no doubt. I had, however, had so much trouble with this paper [the second] that . . . I was discouraged. The Geological Survey had fallen into the hands of small men, and was no longer the grand institution that it was in the days when Major Powell was its Director. The policy seemed to be to set up captious criticism and obstruct the scientific work of members of the staff. It was a case of bureaucracy. There was no longer any *esprit de corps,* and no one was certain that his work would be approved by petty officers at headquarters.[33]

Instead, Ward's dictionary work, with no one to watch over his shoulder, earned more money and provided greater time to continue his writings in sociology, which were producing greater recognition than his efforts in paleobotany. In 1903, Ward had published *Pure Sociology,* which was based upon his classification of all sciences into the two categories, pure and applied.[34] And his successful trip to Europe that summer visiting Continental sociologists, along with an offer by James Dealey of Brown University to prepare a textbook on sociology from his earlier works, had reinforced his preference for social science.

Consequently, in January 1905, after having spent most of 1904 in dictionary work and in writing the manuscript for *Applied Sociology,* his sequel to *Pure Sociology,* Ward resigned from the survey. By mid-1905, *Applied Sociology* was finished, though not yet published, to complete Ward's system of sociology. When the book appeared in 1906, it proved to be Ward's best seller in a progressive era that was responsive to the spirit of his reform arguments—if not to his antiquated literary construction.[35] Yet his theme in *Applied Sociology* remained the same as it had been in 1883: the efficacy of widespread human intelligence to direct the natural and social forces of the world for the improved happiness of man.

Evidence in Ward's life of at least the personal validity of his doctrine began to appear in 1905. The initiative shown by social science professor James Dealey of Brown University brought about the publication of a synopsis of *Dynamic Sociology, Psychic Factors,* and *Pure Sociology* in a tightened form that was more accessible to student minds and that sold at a price better suited to their purses. The result, *A Text-Book of Sociology,* promised to provide a wider hearing for Ward's views than had his earlier books.[36] In Professor Dealey, moreover, Ward found a disciple and confidant; and this friendship was important since Albion Small had fallen into Ward's disfavor by his acceptance of a critical review of *Pure Sociology* in the *American Journal of Sociology*.[37]

Dealey invited Ward to Providence as early as 1904 to lecture to the local Women's Club and to discuss Ward's ideas. It was Dealey, along with Charles William August Veditz of George Washington University, who arranged a December 1905 plenary session at Providence for a breakaway faction of sociologists from the American Economic Association. Uneasy over the academic imperialism of the economists and at least superficially certain of a scientific foundation for a separate social science, this group of the foremost East Coast sociologists formed the American Sociology Society on December 27. Apparently to Ward's surprise, he was elected president instead of Franklin Giddings of Columbia. "I never was so much taken aback in my life," wrote Ward.[38]

VIII   *A New Call For An Old Man*

Soon after his election as president of the American Sociology Society, Dealey and George Wilson, the other member of the small social science department at Brown University, urged their president, William Faunce, to invite Ward to a new professorship of sociology at the school. Because Ward had an international reputation as a sociologist, because he had just been honored by the American Sociological Society election, and because his bearing and manner—if not all his ideas—were amply dignified, he was thought to be acceptable to Brown. Moreover, he would probably come for a small stipend; and conservative Brown, which had not yet joined other universities around the country in establishing a sociology position, could utilize his expertise. President Faunce saw the wisdom of their case and the splendid opportunity to add to the prestige of the university at little expense. The sixty-five-year-old Ward was delighted with Faunce's invitation in the spring of 1906 to join the Brown faculty, for he regarded the position as one more sinecure to provide not only a livelihood during his remaining years but also an opportunity to increase the currency of his ideas. Surprisingly, no one seemed to recognize the irony

of having religious iconoclast Ward—whose economic and sexual
views were also less than orthodox—join one of the more conservative church-related Ivy League schools that had an un-
inspiring record for academic freedom.

After spending the summer in Europe, the new professor and
his wife returned to Brown to take up lodgings. Rose's health,
however, broke early during their first year in Providence; she
returned to Washington to be nursed by her sister, Sarah Comstock; and in 1908 a severe stroke paralyzed her. In order to
economize on his two thousand dollar salary, Ward moved into
one of the student rooming houses.

At Brown Ward was a respected professor, although many
students who believed a course under him "the thing" to do
had difficulty comprehending his broad-ranging lectures in his
course "A Survey of All Knowledge." At the end of his first
year, Ward's students presented him with a loving cup; and
in 1912 they dedicated the school yearbook to the white-haired
old man in the Parisian slouch hat whose rugged physique now
betrayed a "scholar's stoop." But the "old man," who had been
on a pension for over half his life for wounds which "incapaci-
tated" him from physical labor, was still taking fifteen mile
hikes from Providence as he traced the geological formation
of the area.

Among his academic colleagues, Ward was respected for his
scholarly reputation, even though he was quite reserved and
seemingly aloof in a situation where he no doubt felt self-
conscious of the difference between him and his associates in
social background and in academic pedigree. As a professor
who shared an office with Ward in Maxcy Hall in 1909 commented, "Ward was not of the academic type."[39] Dealey, Wilson,
and Harry Koopman, the Brown librarian with whom Ward
shared a love of books, constituted his only close friends at
Brown. Nonetheless, Ward's years of playing bureaucratic games
in Washington had well-equipped him for survival at Brown,
and the fact that he was truly gratified to have found the
professorship that had eluded him throughout his earlier life
pleased him and aided his adjustment. President Faunce handled
Ward with skilled diplomacy, and his public praise of Ward
kept the old man assured of the wisdom of the administration.

The new professor jealously met his classes, and he was careful to arrange his public speaking so that it would not interfere with his teaching. He was just as rigorous in attending daily chapel; in fact, Faunce, in chastising publicly other faculty members, commended Ward in 1909 for his regular attendance. On that occasion the still fully alert Ward nudged the professor next to him and remarked, "I deserve no credit for it, as the servant is cleaning up my room at this hour."[40]

While Ward's religious views had at least moderated to the point where he could tolerate Baptist sermons, his politico-economic and social views had, if anything, become more radical. Socialism in the United States and in Great Britain had almost become respectable, and reforms of all sorts were in the air. Individual socialists and a surge of Socialist educational forums paid court to Ward, and he spoke to various Socialist groups in America and abroad. Eugene Debs and lesser organizers quoted Ward in speeches and pamphlets, and Ward even found himself at speakers' tables with Emma Goldman, the well-known Anarchist.

Ward's summer visiting professorships at Columbia, Wisconsin, and Chicago and also his visits to Europe in 1909 and 1911 to represent Brown at international academic affairs and to pursue his interest in European sociology provided him in his remaining years with the sense of achievement that he had desired so much throughout his life. Yet the incapacity and absence of his wife upon whom he had depended for companionship, along with the unfamiliar and socially exclusive atmosphere of Brown, left Ward rather lonely. Because of his loneliness, Ward turned increasingly after 1908 to the idea of compiling a "mental autobiography." This work was to contain not only all of his published articles and lesser writings but also autobiographical commentaries that would show readers the development of his thought.

Happily for Ward's hopes of compiling such "glimpses of the cosmos," as he tentatively entitled the series, Mrs. Emily Palmer Cape was attracted into his orbit. Ward had always been a handsome and virile man, and his writings and lectures since the 1880's had championed the women's rights movement. These traits, combined with his public reputation, produced a group of women admirers. Indeed, more than half of the letters he received came from married and from professional women who for various reasons, but especially because of his free thought and women's rights views, found him interesting company. After he began teaching special summer classes and extension courses in the 1890's and after his popular writings about sex became better known, the number of such women admirers increased; and Emily Palmer Cape was one such woman. At forty-five, the mother of two nearly grown children, the wife of a well-to-do New York businessman, and an aspiring writer-philosopher, she needed something meaningful to do—and Ward was her solution. Mrs. Cape's Transcendental ideas were not incompatible with Ward's free thought, and she found herself anxious for the expanded education that he encouraged in his writings.

In 1905, she initiated a formal correspondence which continued until 1908 when she visited him at Providence. In person, she encouraged his idea of compiling his lesser known writings; and, since he had no secretarial help for the considerable work involved in preparing his papers and comments for publication, Mrs. Cape volunteered to do the more routine work at her home. By 1910, Ward became a frequent houseguest and a friend of the family. That summer Mrs. Cape followed Ward to Madison, Wisconsin, and took a boardinghouse room next to his to facilitate their joint efforts at putting his papers into order while he lectured at the University of Wisconsin. The next year Mrs. Cape, who knew President Nicholas Murray Butler of Columbia University, arranged for Ward to teach a summer class there and to live with the Capes while their collaboration continued. In the meantime, Ward agreed that, after his papers had been edited, Mrs. Cape would have use of them and of his life-long diaries in order to prepare his biography.

Ward's relationship with Mrs. Cape was unconventional, but scanty proof exists of the illicit affair that was suspected by Sarah Comstock of Washington who was caring for the bedridden Rose. Since Ward's full agenda left time for only holiday visits to Washington, his sociologist niece, Miss Sarah Simons— the same age as Mrs. Cape—was as displeased as her aunt with the amount of time he spent with the New York woman. A few notes and slips of paper in Ward's newspaper file, which survived the thorough search by the two Sarahs after Ward's death, are all that remain to reconstruct the "wonderful and beautiful friendship" between Ward and Cape—and all of them were written by Mrs. Cape.[41] In them, she speaks of long walks with Ward, of an occasional kiss under the trees, and of the secret love affair of George Eliot. Although Ward was pleased with the infatuation of this younger woman and with the considerable attention she provided in preparing his manuscript, no other evidence of his reaction to, or his relationship with her exists.

In late March 1913, Ward left Brown early for his Easter vacation in Washington in an effort to recoup his failing health. On April 17, a copy of the first volume of *Glimpses of the Cosmos* arrived in the mail which immensely pleased the ailing scholar; the next day, Ward suffered a heart attack and died. After his burial in Washington, Mrs. Comstock and Miss Simons completed the editing of *Glimpses of the Cosmos,* reduced its scope from twelve to six volumes, and deleted all references to Mrs. Cape in the concluding volumes. After going through Ward's papers in order to insure the reputation of their sister and aunt and to frustrate any future biography by Mrs. Cape, the two burned over forty notebook diaries that Ward had kept. As a result of this "temporary insanity," as one of Ward's students wrote, or "Dastardly Deed!" as Mrs. Cape viewed the incident, the two women left intact only his first diaries from 1860 to 1870—the years before he had met Rose Simons Pierce.[42] So Ward, who throughout his life had wavered between public controversy and bureaucratic caution, was stilled.

CHAPTER 2

Education: The Great Panacea

I Sources of Ward's Ideas On Education

LESTER Ward's dreams of a public education system that
would serve as a democratic force in American society
was an effort, like that of so many American reform movements
between 1865 and 1914, to transpose earlier values and practices of a largely rural and economically mobile life to a significantly altered urban and industrial society:

> I can vividly recall [Ward reminisced] that when myself a pupil
> in the public schools of my own village there were some boys in
> attendance who belonged to the lowest classes. . . . There were also
> in attendance some of the sons of the wealthy men of the place. All
> were placed on a common level in the school, and the only test
> of merit was ability to recite the lessons. And I remember the genuine
> satisfaction that it afforded me frequently to see the poor boys "beat"
> the rich ones and "go to the head," and I began to see even at that
> tender age that all was not gold that glittered.[1]

As Ward's testimony suggests, the powerful force of class motiva-
tion caused him to view education as a principal class-leveler
that could develop the egalitarian features of American society
that had been his own hope for advancement.

Nowhere else in the late nineteenth century does one find a
more articulate spokesman than Ward for the American dream
of opportunity or a more authentic example of the power of
America's traditional social myth to produce results. But, without
Ward's equal commitment to an ethic of work and the expanding
nature of the American economy, the dream might have completely withered. As it was, Ward's advancements and successes
were slow in coming; and he was commonly frustrated by the

abyss between his expectations and his achievements. Nonetheless, such unconscious emotional intensity and such conscious intellectual articulation kept the nation's reform commitment to publicly supported opportunity for the underside of American society from disappearing. In an age of increased class differentiation, new aggregations of oligarchic economic and political power, and intellectual theories of Naturalistic Determinism that undermined earlier democratic assumptions, Ward's stubborn refusal to abandon the dreams of his youth, while harnessing early-nineteenth-century democratic and work ethics to the intellectual respectability of the new evolutionary sciences, kept alive a vital element in the American consciousness.

Knowledge was power, status, and achievement combined in one; and the short essay, "Read and You Will Know," from a McGuffey's reader haunted Ward's mind like a ceaseless refrain. The theme dominated an oration given by Ward in his early days as a government clerk in Washington, D. C. Before the Concordia Lyceum in 1866, the ambitious young bureaucrat spoke on "The Independence of Thought" to other clerks like himself who were prone to agree that education and cultural background were the differences between themselves and their political superiors.[2] A similar conviction motivated Ward's long labors from 1869 to 1876 in writing a treatise about the value of education—one significantly titled "The Great Panacea." While the manuscript was largely abandoned in the mid-1870's for a more scientific analysis based on his college readings, the resulting *Dynamic Sociology* (1883) concluded that education, as a "panacea," was really a law of nature demonstrated by the operations of evolution.

Ward's new approach to education was greatly influenced by August Comte, the French Positivist philosopher, who earlier in the century had attempted to reform society by replacing theological and metaphysical explanations of man and society with the findings of the modern positive sciences. In order to accomplish Comte's sweeping intellectual and social reform, Ward believed it was necessary to diffuse information, especially scientific information, throughout society; and this popularization of knowledge was the major responsibility of schools in a dynamic society. Such schooling, he believed, would fully open the broadly based talents of formerly submerged populations and would, thereby, make possible the full opportunity promised by American democratic ideals. Individual Americans would find greater happiness in the satisfaction of self-development and in the comforts produced by an increased control of nature's resources, while society, too, would gain by an accelerated rate of social evolution that was shared by all its members.

Ward's faith in education rested, like that of Horace Mann a generation earlier, on a closely related faith in the perfectibility of human life and social institutions through effort and environmental control. Not surprisingly, both Mann and Ward accepted the principle of acquired hereditarian characteristics espoused by Jean Lamarck, the French botanist, as a scientific basis for educational theory in a democratic republic. Like William James, Lester Ward found Naturalistic Determinism, a rival social theory likewise based on evolutionary science, quite unacceptable to both his scientific findings and his educational faith. Mind and intelligence, Ward believed, did not merely adapt to an exterior world as the determinists claimed; for such qualities could change that environment if their possessors so desired. Prerational men adapted to the environment; rational men transformed it.

In educational theory, as in nearly all other matters, Ward defined himself by taking a position contrary to his English social-evolutionary adversary, Herbert Spencer. Spencer's ideological commitment to laissez-faire Individualism and his own fortunate experience of family tutoring placed him in direct opposition to Ward's program for social progress through compulsory public education. On scarcely no other issue were the battle lines between Ward and Spencer so firmly drawn; and Ward seldom failed to indicate that, contrary to popular belief, Spencer was neither self-educated nor a self-made man. He was the product of extensive family instruction, of a wide exposure to important books and periodicals, and of close personal acquaintance with leaders of British intellectual life. If such intellectual stimulation could be organized and provided for all children—in contrast to Ward's own random education—then social competence and intellectual gains for society would be proportional to the added mental stimulation. Spencer's advocacy of private home study was sharply attacked by Ward for its assumption that every child had parents and friends capable of educating him. While this had been true for Spencer, Ward knew from his own experience that the economic and educational backgrounds of only a minority of families could support such a plan. As the methods and content of education improved, Ward suggested, the students would educate the parents.

Ward was an avid reader of Spencer, and in condensed form he attempted in *Dynamic Sociology* to parallel Spencer's extended system of philosophy; but his social conclusions were more in accord with his own Activist faith in the efficacy of education to promote social reform. Ward and Spencer agreed that evolution during the greatest part of early human existence had functioned as a planless, slow-moving, genetic development. But, during this course of natural selection, Ward insisted, the mind had developed as an indirect means of maximizing pleasure and of improving the quality of reproduction. In the case of humans, the mind had developed sufficiently for men to grasp an understanding of how evolution functioned. By understanding the laws of nature, men might harness them to human objectives just as they had gained control and use of nature through an understanding of the laws of physics. Consequently, education, viewed by Ward as an understanding of the laws of nature, was the most important of essential human activities and was worthy of the greatest concern of men individually and collectively.

II *Education As The Basis For Social Progress*

Ward's commitment to universal public education stemmed in large part from his own class position and from his desire to insure that working people were given the respect and opportunity that he desired for himself. His social reform thought, consequently, is to a considerable extent an outgrowth of his early analysis of what would best serve his own needs. The extraordinary valuation given to achievement by Ward prompted him to view education, provided by a popularly controlled state, as the most likely means of achieving his personal goals and of promoting social progress.

His own eventual success and that of the nation in the years following the Civil War led Ward to find a law of progress running through nature. That law of progress had its most favorable environment in the United States, he believed, where every man's mind was given the opportunity for development and expression. Ward's pride in nationality, so clear in the aftermath of his participation in the war and his employment by the government, had appeared earlier in a Pennsylvania school essay that pointed out the superiority of the United States to all other countries because of its "general diffusion of the means of education throughout its territories."[3] There was no need for revolution in America; what was necessary was human direction of the progressive evolution of her institutions.

"The spirit of the present age may be said to be Progress," wrote Ward as he identified his own upward movement with that of American society.[4] Progress, he declared, consisted in increasing the facilities for the intercommunication of ideas among men and in augmenting their power to extract from nature more of the necessities of life. In either case, knowledge of nature was essential for improved technique. Modern scientific civilization increased happiness by relieving the burdens of men, by substituting mechanical for muscular force, by cheapening and improving commodities, and by gratifying desires.

More importantly, the increased knowledge of the present worked to "enlarge the views, elevate the thoughts, liberalize the sentiments, and extend universal charity and fraternal feeling."[5] If education were withdrawn, however, the complicated machinery of civilization would slow to a crawl and degeneracy would shortly begin. Progress, then, was by no means stable or inevitable; it was frequently threatened with a total eclipse by the rise of erroneous belief that was incompatible with progress. This possibility was an important reason for holding a correct opinion about evolution; for an idea of fixity in the universe produced an attitude of fixity in the mind and toward change, while correct ideas about evolution gave the mind an impulse to move with the tide of progress. Ideas, then, fully as much as technical advances, provided the motive force for progress.

Ward's arguments supporting education as the best means

of promoting social progress, at the same time that it advanced personal opportunity, are found in virtually all of his works. His most popular statement of this traditional American democratic doctrine is found in a *Forum* article of the 1880's, "Broadening the Way to Success," which served as a frequent lecture topic for Ward, containing, as he wrote in his autobiography, "the root idea of my entire philosophy of human progress, as I have always held it since my schoolboy days."[6] Ward's elaboration of the familiar multiple merits of universal public education was couched in an argument based upon scientific biology and democratic political theory. Theories of genius that were founded on internal elements of heredity were viewed by Ward as "aristocratic," but attention to enriching the environmental external factors of nurture and education for all people was the "democratic" path of action. Since he held that each class of people contained within it similar degrees of intellectual potential, "what modern society most needs is to abolish this god Genius, to dethrone the monarch Success, to do away with the present oligarchy of brains, and to establish a true democracy of ideas, based upon an equal chance for all."[7]

Education, he contended, should be in a comprehensive form, not limited strictly to traditional schools, but designed to place individuals under a changed environment favorable to the development of all their faculties. Ward never spelled out the details of such an alteration of environment, but the implications were enormous. Society for its own benefit had nothing less than the opportunity to shape its conditions of life to produce the human and social characteristics that in the past had existed only in the dreams of utopians.

In a new progressive society as much support for public education would have to be mobilized as there had been for religious education in the past. Hopefully, believed Ward, the school would replace the church; scientific lectures, the sermon; and the study of natural objects and scientific works would substitute for that of sacred writings. The chasm between the intelligent few and the ignorant many would have to be bridged, just as earlier reformers had preached the need to bridge the gap between the working and the middle classes. The masses would have to be educated about their own interests; for, if they did not comprehend how changes could benefit them, they would always block progress. Indeed, the uneducated provided much of the support for anti-intellectualism in America; the ignorant denounced intelligence, tried to prevent it from infecting them, and designing demagogues manipulated such people for the benefit of those who controlled existing education. Consequently, a basic change in public opinion was necessary, Ward insisted, to right the power balance and to free people from their intellectual bondage.

Since education was power, as Ward contended, those without it were at the mercy of their enlightened fellows. In other power-oriented reform movements of the day, from the anti-monopolist Greenbackers of the 1870's to the Populists of the 1890's, power had been equated with money; and various theories had been devised to explain the evils of economic monopoly. Ward simply replaced these economic terms with those of education. So just as Henry George had decried the unfair advantage of those who lived off the unearned increment of property rents, Ward attacked those whose monopoly of education allowed them power and advantage over people who by reasons of family poverty were unable to secure the knowledge necessary for opportunity. The problem lay not in the production of knowledge, but in its distribution. The monopoly could be broken, in Ward's analysis, through the intervention of government led by individuals who understood the power of education.

While Ward is most easily understood as a social reformer who thought of education as a social device to stimulate progressive social adaptations by society, he can at the same time be viewed as a proponent of basically conservative social values. Ward's fundamental conservatism in liberal dress appeared in some of the results he believed universal education would produce. While he castigated education designed solely for discipline, he clearly assumed that study would produce inner self-discipline, an orderly life, and the work habits that had sustained him personally and that had led him to generalize about the psychic and social advantages of the traditional American work ethic. Furthermore, since public education was a product of government, Ward expected that students who found personal happiness and social usefulness from its incul-

cation would take increased interest in governmental processes
and would give their support to the government that had
liberated their lives.

In Ward's theory, as in his life, work assumed a psychological
and ethical dimension far beyond purely economic considerations.
Certainly his life exemplified the work ethic taught by the
physical necessities and rural mores of mid-nineteenth-century
America. Enthusiasm for work and drive for education were
inseparable as Ward understood his experience. "We are determined to become wise," he declared in January 1869, in balancing
the past year's accounts and setting down in his diary his plans
for the coming year.[8] "What I need now is to read the great
authors and make many scientific experiments. If I could cover
the other professions of medicine and theology and learn two
more languages, Hebrew and Spanish, it would help me a great
deal." He and Lizzie were attempting to comply with a stagger-
ing work agenda: formal classes in the evenings, language study
at work, conjugating Greek verbs while walking to and from
the treasury office, and reading encyclopedias in his leisure time.
This compulsive search for knowledge seems to have moved
beyond a sober calculation for advancement into a compensatory
emotional satisfaction for his successive delays and temporary
failures in becoming first a college student, later a lawyer, and
finally a college professor. To Ward, work was an escape as
well as a future promise.

This conservative side of Ward's educational theory supporting
traditional values of the work ethic and of national patriotism
should not, however, obscure the fact that Ward had in mind
a nationally sponsored education that would enable diligent
students to produce the material and emotional enhancements
of human life. The old order was not by any means to be
completely jettisoned, but those personal qualities revered by
Ward and the inherited knowledge of Western culture were
to be applied teleologically to usher in an improved society
beyond accurate description by contemporary seers. Nor was
Ward in his educational reform theories opposed to institutions,
for he believed that through enlightened institutions man could
organize the knowledge and power necessary to achieve his
objectives. Man's "natural self" was no *summa bonum* for Ward,

for he was convinced that the subordination of nature and of man's "natural self" had enabled him through genetic evolution to leave slowly his savagery and to reach his current stage of civilization. The rationality, efficiency, and economy of energy that had become the values of a new industrial order promised, therefore, to be equally beneficial when applied to the institutions of public education.

III   *Educational Theory*

Progressive education, as Laurence Cremin notes, was an effort to apply the promise of American life to the hard realities of urban-industrial life.[9] In a variety of ways by the turn of the century, reform educators were attempting to inject new life into moribund schools. Of the four criteria suggested by Cremin to identify these early initiatives in progressive education, Ward's theory fully meets three, but it differs sharply with a fourth. Ward believed that pedagogical principles should be derived from the new scientific research in the natural and social sciences; and, as a social scientist himself, he also believed that education should be broadened to apply to the health, the vocations, and the community life of students. Furthermore, he had full faith that all Americans could share in the benefits of democratized education without lowering American culture. At a theoretical level, however, Ward did not agree with the view of some later progressive educators that instruction should be tailored to meet the presumed different needs of various classes of children being brought into public education. On the contrary, Ward insisted on equal accessibility to the common store of man's hard-won store of knowledge. Despite this difference, it seems quite clear that various reformers who, like Ward, were driven by conviction and hopes, yet restrained by conventional notions of political and social propriety, found in education a socially acceptable and practical means of achieving the promise of American life.

Ward's personal educational theory began and ended with a social conclusion drawn from the doctrine of evolution: environment had nearly unlimited power to mold the organism. The issue, Ward contended, was whether the social system should always be left to nature and allowed to drift listlessly on, or whether it should be treated as a subject of art by human intelligence that was as superior to nature as artificial products were generally superior to natural ones. His long concluding chapter in the second volume of *Dynamic Scoiology* was devoted to education as the summation of man's knowledge of natural history and his social means for future evolution.

Education, Ward wrote, was a systematic process for manufacturing the correct opinions that underlay all conduct. The data of opinions was knowledge, hence the necessity for the equal distribution of the extant knowledge of the world for the broadest diffusion of correct opinion. Education was an artificial system for assorting impressions, providing a systematic presentation of data, and employing indirect natural forces to do what would otherwise be laborious work. Natural forces were not to be rejected, even the harmful ones, nor could they be destroyed. Rather, men, by knowing the properties of such natural forces, could guide them into useful channels, just as the millwright employed the gravitational power of water running downhill. Although education was a slow process since it worked through indirection, it was the only practicable method at hand for improving human happiness by enabling men to gain greater intellectual and physical control of nature.

In order to utilize education as a principal instrument for increasing human happiness, Ward outlined three major requirements for any system of education. First, the principal concern of education should be with the contents of the mind, not its capacity. Second, education should be exclusively the work of society operating through the state. And third, education had to be universal. In regard to the capacity of the human mind, Ward, contrary to some public belief, maintained that it was impossible for the brain to be worn out by acquiring large amounts of knowledge. People were as capable of absorbing useful and reliable information as the burdens of trivia that belabored most minds. The common village gossip, he remarked, held, perhaps from memory, as much antisocial information in his head as the most famous scientist held reliable and socially useful knowledge. Concern should not rest, therefore, with arguments about the capacity of human brains—the preoccupation of aristocratic theorists and eugenicists—but with the acquisition of reliable and sufficient content.

The methodology of science, wrote Ward, anticipating the pragmatists, taught a reliable means of establishing knowledge for use in the schools. While the method was infallible, the conclusions were conditional; facts could be known absolutely only if all other conditions relative to the subject were known to be true. No proposition should be accepted until it had been satisfactorily established by thorough scientific analysis. Knowledge in the past had been determined very slowly from countless repetitions of natural experience. In the future, through the application of scientific methodology, it would become a teleological manufacture. Once the inequalities in the distribution of knowledge were eliminated, the inequalities of condition that currently existed would disappear, leaving only the natural differences of human capacity.[10]

What especially characterized men in historic times was that they had found means of preserving their inheritance of knowledge and had been able to add to it, making the whole process cumulative. Culturally speaking, this inheritance constituted the "social germ plasm," analogous to the continuity of genetic germ plasm discovered by August Weismann. In its fashion, the social germ plasm of knowledge was likewise immortal; but, unlike the automatic transmission of the physical germ plasm, it was absolutely necessary that conscious, directed effort be made by society to pass on the accumulated body of knowledge to each new generation. "Organic and social heredity are not the same and cannot be interchanged," wrote Ward, who was criticizing the conservative social organicists who applied deterministic biological theory to society.[11] The supreme duty of civilized man was to maintain the continuity of the *social* germ plasm, he argued, clearly distinguishing himself from the eugenic and race-oriented social theorists. "This knowledge, wrought by toil and struggle, by patience and thought, by genius and skill, and heaped up little by little through ages of time, is the Promethean fire that must never be allowed to go out."[12]

Despite the basic importance of knowledge through education, Ward observed, the nature of all previous societies and governments had limited its acquisition to a mere handful of people.

Ignoring the possible logic of an economic interpretation of this history, Ward theorized that this limitation on education was itself a direct result of the relative lack of knowledge that had led men to ignore the potential benefits of a broad diffusion of information. It was not necessary, of course, for all people to absorb every parcel of information. Rather, by careful classification of information—Ward's methodological panacea in education as in science—it was possible to reduce the practical truths of all knowledge so that they would be within the power of the overwhelming majority of minds to comprehend and to apply.

Theoretically, different types of public education could be employed with success; but such detailed planning was not Ward's intention. Nonetheless, he argued, the history of the United States suggested that education in the hands of the state—society in its collective capacity—was most successful in organizing and directing the transmission of the social germ plasm. Ecclesiastical and private efforts were either too limited or too narrow to work for the general good of society. Religious parochial education was particularly ill-suited for the task because of the sectarian admission requirements and the doctrinal distortions of subject matter imposed by particular religious biases. While Ward's opposition to parochial education was originally directed almost entirely against the Catholic Church, his increasingly agnostic position by the late 1860's led him to suspect any religiously sponsored schools. Only secular public education, he insisted, made possible a truly open search for truth. Since democratic government represented the entire society, it was less likely to be hampered by traditional ideas— and errors—than were religious institutions that rested on revealed truth and on entrenched privileges.

In spite of Ward's inside knowledge of the weaknesses of "Gilded Age" Washington, he still believed that there were sufficient men of talent and conscience within the national bureaucracy to plan responsibly for a public system of education. Government always administered more effectively than it legislated, claimed the lifelong bureaucrat. While no state had yet fully realized the general diffusion of knowledge among its citizenry, democratic governments had moved closest to the

objective. Initially supporting elementary education through public resources, the United States now promised through high
schools and state universities to deliver better education to the
masses than the privately endowed institutions in the past had
provided for the privileged few.

State education, moreover, could compel education for those
ignorant of their own interests who would not otherwise attend
private schools. Ironically, those who needed education most
desired it the least; and those whose poverty required it could
ill afford it. Both groups would be best served by the prestige
and financial resources of the state. Public schools would insure,
furthermore, that the children of wealthy parents received no
special favors. Private education, unfortunately, was often worse
than none at all since it increased the inequality in existing
intelligence and intensified the distance between classes. An
uneducated class, Ward pointed out, was an expensive class
since everyone had to pay for the crime and welfare costs it
created. Since that class could not be annihilated and since
such people would not civilize themselves, society had to
reclaim them through education. For the major social commitment necessary to educate the masses, only the power and the
influence of the state would suffice.

Ward's insistence on the universal appropriation of education
rested on his faith in the ability of common men to profit from
such a benefit. A radical idea in the late nineteenth century,
it continued to be so for many people long into the twentieth.
Ward's faith in man was a function of his monistic understanding of the operation of nature. Throughout the universe,
he argued, insisting upon a cosmic rationale for his ideas, there
existed latent potential that required only proper environmental
conditions for its release in creative activity.

IV *Specific Applications of Education*

Ward never developed specific curriculums or courses of
study; but, although he preferred the higher ground of principle,
he did comment on the selection of knowledge to be taught
in his proposed universal public schools. In order to assist
teachers and to insure a high quality education throughout a

nation, Ward advocated a national curriculum formulated by educational experts who would also establish model systems of grading. In addition, similar authorities should compile treatises on the subject matter and pedagogy of the public schools that would be in conformity with society's telic objectives. Following the logic of his nationalizing enthusiasm, Ward also suggested the establishment of a national university to be located in Washington, D. C. The existing scientific bureaus of government, he proposed, could form the foundation for a model university which could also carry on the necessary research work upon which the government relied. Undoubtedly Ward saw in such a plan the likelihood of a major university appointment which had so far in his life eluded him, but his concept fit very neatly into his own views of the necessary nationalizing of public education with Washington D. C., as much the center of educational ideas and programs as the Geological Survey was in the field of science.

In considering the most advantageous environment for the development of students, Ward was drawn into the emerging urban-rural controversy. Ward recognized merit in both sides of the dispute, and he characteristically adopted a position not unlike that of his personal background. Once again Ward was tempted to find cosmic law to justify his own experience. Remembering the chances for intellectual growth in the villages of Illinois and Iowa, Ward was struck by the more favorable educational environment provided by cities. People of talent in rural areas, he warned, would have to gravitate to the cities or else lose any opportunity for recognition and development. In fact, so essential were the circumstances of the city for intellectual stimulation that he found them "the indispensable conditions to any and all progress beyond mediocrity."[13] Buoyed by his own life in Washington, Ward pointed particularly to the coming together of people with similar intellectual interests in the new urban centers; the opportunities for contacts, discussion, and access to libraries; the economic resources which insured security and leisure for research; and the greater number of urban vocations that utilized the challenging fields of intellectual life.

Though remorseful at times about his slow start in educated

life, Ward on other occasions found positive consolation for his
early rural years. In "Early Education and Precocity," written
in the 1890's, he argued that parents should ensure that their
children be given a basic encounter with nature early in life
to arouse their natural curiosity and to acquaint them with the
real world of life.[14] Generations of life in cities, he claimed in
Lamarckian terms of inheritance, would breed children mentally
and morally effete. Man had evolved in a natural setting, and
he needed to maintain that contact, particularly in his early
years. Because of the advantages of a rural childhood, Ward
suggested that urban kindergartens could keep children without
exposure to books until the age of ten as long as the youngsters
were given direct experience with nature to enrich the lifeless
and stale atmosphere of the city. City school systems, at the
very least, should avail themselves fully of parks, suburban
excursions, and outdoor sports.

As for formal subject matter, Ward encouraged personal contact with the substance of a subject; but "literature," in the
limited sense of explanatory and interpretive writing, was regarded by him as quite necessary, especially for those who had
to move rapidly against the early obstacles of limited contact
with knowledge. Observation and experience were desirable,
but they could never replace the necessity for printed matter
that abstracted from the relatively slow and wasteful method
of education gained solely from natural experience. Those who
had hoarded precious school readers in the bookless central
prairies could not be misled by fanciful tales of the superiority
of the natural man or of the subversion of the natural instincts
by book learning. Nevertheless, such printed literature was the
vehicle, promoter, and conservator of knowledge; it was not the
substance of knowledge itself.

Fiction, on the other hand, as a particular form of literature,
most commonly manipulated pleasing fantasies of empty content and consequently produced no redeeming social content.
From Ward's vantage point, this waste of time and paper in
fiction was particularly true of the sentimental romances of his
day. On one occasion Ward swept out of a club meeting when
the discussion turned to a contemporary literary controversy,
remarking that he had time neither to read nor to discuss such

trivia. "What is called polite and classic literature of the world consists in adroit ways of saying nothing," he remarked. "Putting that of all languages together, there is not truth enough in it all to have kept civilization from perishing if it had depended solely upon it for its stock of information."[15] Novels of strong social reform content, like those of Charles Dickens and Victor Hugo, were exempted by Ward; the reading of these novels of social protest brought him to tears, as the stories touched the still sensitive emotional memory of his early years. Later in life, Ward's caustic literal-mindedness mellowed some, and he made room for the usefulness of esthetic writings to stimulate the senses. The change in attitude was largely geared to the increasing frequency of social novels in European and American literature. Fine arts devoted to action and social reform, he admitted "not only may become, but in a great degree have already become, a dynamic factor in society."[16]

Ward's openness to subjects that attracted his personal attention, irrespective of their popular acceptance, caused him to recommend curriculum innovations that had considerable merit. Sex education, for example, based on important functions of mankind, should not be slighted, he maintained, because of sentimental values. But the limits and dangers of Ward's own preferences in defining model curriculums for a national educational system were just as pronounced as his projected reforms. His early repugnance for mathematics, for example, led him to minimize its importance except as a tool for learning "real" knowledge. Particularly detested by Ward was the argument that mathematics developed mental discipline; he retorted that exclusive mathematical study destroyed both the reason and the judgment "because it consists in prolonged thinking about nothing."[17]

Moreover, the one thing that was to be avoided in schoolwork, wrote Ward in discussing curriculums, was specialization—at least until the most advanced classes were reached. Overspecialization, the widely read scientist wrote, led to a narrowness of outlook, to a special arrogance, and to a tendency to make erroneous judgments about subjects in areas outside one's isolated field. If a person aspired to be knowledgeable in a variety of fields, Ward advised, he must at least distill the general truths of each. A broadly educated public, not a narrow technocracy, was his objective: "I have entirely given up hope that specialists will ever be imbued with many of the great truths that science teaches. They are not in search of truth, but only of facts.... The hope is in the general educated public, who, having no specialties to absorb and narrow them, are interested in all science and all truth."[18] His personal effort to combat the fragmentation of knowledge in and by his Brown University course, "A Survey of All Knowledge," seemed presumptuous, if not preposterous, to those who did not understand his concept of "knowledge," and the course did not survive his death.

If the evils of specialization which Ward accurately foresaw were to be avoided, and if all people were to be exposed to at least the general truths of all fields of knowledge, education in its various forms would have to become more popularized in its presentation. To support the popularization of science, Ward encouraged the public, and particularly Frederick Law Olmstead, the landscape architect of the Washington Capitol grounds, to preserve the Rock Creek Park area as a national park for the study of nature. While Ward's influence on Olmstead was only one of many, and Ward himself never claimed major credit, Olmstead did use Ward's flora guides and quoted his work on the Rock Creek area in his successful efforts to protect the botany and beauty of the park from the ax and the plow. In a similar vein, Ward authored a report in 1900 about the fossil tree beds of northwest Arizona which was used by John F. Lacey, chairman of the House of Representatives public lands committee, to have the area declared a national monument by Congress for the use of paleobotanical research and public learning.[19] When the popularization of science and the availability of living laboratories for the public were promoted particularly well by national government scientists and agencies, Ward found his more general theory about nationalized education confirmed by his experience.

Ward's popular education emphasis found support and acceptance from two particular groups who felt themselves disadvantaged by their lack of education and the lack of power that accompanied that disability. These two groups were culturally mobile middle class women and ambitious, urban working class young men. From the 1880's until his death, Ward received numerous letters from women who found hope for their aspirations in his scientific-sounding arguments for public education. Most of his female correspondents found hope in Ward's educational theories for their own ambitions and for their escape from the frustrations of their limited social roles. To explain these frustrations, Ward held that current education offered inadequate opportunity to discover and free one's talents. Psychologically, such an explanation was satisfying and most certainly contained substantial truth. As for those who failed to satisfy their own expectations within the accepted achievement-success mythology of American social values, increased education provided an acceptable alternative to the abandonment of either the democratic success ideology or the socioeconomic institutions of American life.

The extent of this support for Ward's educational beliefs among upwardly mobile, mildly liberal middle class women was indicated by the "great enthusiasm" that greeted an address by Mrs. John F. Ottley of Atlanta during the 1897 annual meeting of the General Federation of Women's Clubs.[20] Mrs. Ottley, a dedicated admirer and correspondent of Ward, linked the educational extension work of the women's clubs not only to the satisfaction of its members but to the very attainment of democracy by American society. Democratic equality, she argued, following Ward's analysis closely, was not one of condition but of opportunity. An obtainable utopia—with an intended slam at the socialists—could be created in a democracy where education was not a luxury but the common inheritance of all. Political democracy of the ballot box, while desirable for all, in recognition of woman's suffrage, was no more important than the opportunity to participate in the increase and diffusion of knowledge throughout society.

Ward's case for opening education to working class youth was well stated, with some irony, in his address to the Phi Beta Kappa chapter of Wellesley in 1912.[21] Speaking to young women of prosperous and gifted backgrounds whose aspirations paradoxically paralleled those of the industrial youth to whom he referred, Ward noted that professional educators had failed to present an education of interest and importance to working

people. Instead, workers and the sons of workers had organized
their own classes at Ruskin College, the Central Labour College,
the Rand School of Social Science, the Neff College of New
York, the School of Social Science in Boston, Minassian's School
in Philadelphia, Ferrer's Modern School, and in the meeting
rooms of the Intercollegiate Socialist Society—all of which Ward
had visited and had given his blessing to, as well as occasional
lectures. The need was great, Ward told his audience of pro-
spective teachers, to approach the live subjects of the day in
the light of science rather than in a spirit of dogmatism.

The most spectacular response from the working class young
men who were encouraged by Ward's democratic educational
theory came from Great Britain. From 1906 to 1909, Ward corresponded with Dennis Hird, a teacher of sociology and evolutionary social theory at Ruskin College, Oxford University.
Ruskin College had strong ties to the British trade union
movement and existed to educate the bright young men of
trade union families. Ward sent numerous reprints of his works
to the grateful Hird who found his school perpetually short of
funds for materials. In 1909, a political and educational quarrel
erupted at Ruskin with the result that Hird and about half the
student body split apart from "the conservative element" to
form the Central Labour College.

Ward, who was scheduled to visit Europe in the summer
of 1909, was invited by Hird to attend a labor educational
convention at the new college. Ward consented and found one
of the warmest receptions of his career. His remarks to the
attentive students were met with "great applause"; and, at the
close of his principal address, they all rose and sang "For He's
a Jolly Good Fellow." In fact, Ward was impressed by the
students as much as they were by the presence of an Establishment scholar with an ideology close to their own.

Ward's "dignity of scientific conviction," one observer at
the scene noted, had provided the assurance that the youth
wished to have about the inevitable rise of the common people
through access to modern education. Ward's struggle through
youth and manhood for an education against economic and
cultural obstacles had reinforced his commitment to educational
opportunity, and so had the experience of working class students

in the aristocratic environment of Oxford affected them. "We hung on like grim death to some of the principles you have laid down for our guidance," wrote a student spokesman to Ward after his visit.[22]

The American's remarks to the gathering of British youth were little different from similar addresses he had given to women's clubs, to black high schools, and to public lyceums.[23] Yet Ward did tailor his comments to the extent of making quite explicit his sympathy for laboring class reform. He skillfully identified with the bias of his audience, but he also attacked the "immediate result" that socialists had unrealistically demanded political action to attain. To Ward, such efforts were doomed to failure since social structures, the products of long social evolution, required substantial time for basic change. Instead, as he apparently persuaded the students, the working class reform that could best produce both immediate gains and longer term structural change was the increase of human intelligence. Instead of the need for increasing mental capacity, as the eugenicists argued, Ward once again contended that the native capacity of all classes was sufficient if it was coupled with the extant knowledge that was the prerogative of the powerful. The great problem confronting society, Ward told the students, was the equalization of opportunity by placing all knowledge in the possession of every man.

V An Evaluation

The influence of Lester Ward's work in education is difficult to assess since education as a means of social reform has had many roots in the American experience. Only among a small handful of nationally known educators is there circumstantial evidence of the limited influence of Ward. And, while the subsequent development of educational practices and ideals would have much in common with Ward's position, there is no accurate or dependable way to show that they stemmed from his thought. Realistically, broader cultural and socioeconomic forces seem a good deal more important in explaining progressive education in America than the writings and lectures of a relatively little-known reformer. Yet Ward's voice for universal public education as a means of personal happiness and of general social progress was raised early and continued throughout his life. The resulting climate of opinion that Ward helped to shape engrained, therefore, his basic objectives and much of his rationale into the continuing democratic theory of education. At the very least, Ward had the wisdom to side with an educational theory that served the interests of an upwardly mobile population in an economically and intellectually expanding society.

Among Ward's closest friends was Edward Allsworth Ross, his nephew by marriage, who made education one of his major means of social control for the future. *Social Control*, his widely read treatise whose title reveals much of the undercurrent of the early Progressive movement, was dedicated "To my Master, Lester F. Ward, Pioneer and Pathfinder in the Study of Society."[24] "Uncle Lester's" ideas appear in Ross's prescription for social advancement in an uprooted industrial society where the older communal techniques of ordering society were no longer useful. Increased reliance in the modern age, Ross professed, must now be placed on artificial, rather than natural, supports for social order. Though Ross did not include a single citation to Ward in the text or in the footnotes, his chapter on "Social Suggestion—Education" reflects much of Ward's thought, even though Ross viewed education much more as manipulation than as liberation. The evolutionary drift from religion to education, Ross argued, as did Ward, required secular civic and moral education to provide the "peace and order" that religion and priests once preserved.

Another close friend of Ward's who shows some of the sociologist's influence was his Washington colleague William Torrey Harris. Harris, well-known superintendent of the St. Louis public schools and leader of a neo-Hegelian philosophical school at Concord, accepted the position of United States commissioner of education in 1889; and he worked in Washington in that post to consolidate and to rationalize educational reforms throughout the nation. While Ward and Harris disagreed about the commissioner's strong Hegelian position, they shared a common interest in using national government influence to expand and to systematize public schools throughout the country. Since both agreed about the absolute necessity of universal public education for a self-governing society and about the potential leadership of the national government in designing and supporting such education, their different theoretical approaches contributed to a lively friendship between them. There is some evidence from Harris that he was influenced by Ward to work toward a sociological foundation for his educational philosophy, rather than for a psychological foundation.[25] His writings from the 1890's, after meeting Ward, most clearly reveal his new sociological interests.

John Dewey, America's best known proponent of progressive education, was likewise acquainted with Ward's work. During his early years establishing the famous Laboratory School at the University of Chicago, Dewey had written a friendly review of Ward's *Psychic Factors of Civilization* (1893).[26] Particularly recommended by Dewey in his review was Ward's theory of the evolution of intelligence and its social implication that the increase in human knowledge made possible an organized social assault on human problems. There is no hard evidence that the points of similarity in their theory were directly related, or that they stemmed from other than common assumptions shared by other American intellectuals. Nevertheless, Dewey's emphasis upon education as the fundamental method of social progress and reform was precisely the same as that made by Ward and by Ward's intellectual companion at the University of Chicago, Albion Small. Dewey and Small were instrumental in placing the University of Chicago, a decade before the University of Wisconsin, in the vanguard of the movement to use American universities to improve a modern, urban-industrial society.

Another educator more directly influenced by Ward was Charles Van Hise, the president of the University of Wisconsin from 1903 to 1918. Van Hise, a member of the Geological Survey from 1883 until 1903, was well acquainted with Ward; and they shared a similar interest in seeking out the fundamental principles that underlay the social problems, as well as the geological formations, of America. As president of the University of Wisconsin, he had close contact with Richard Ely in the economics department and with Edward Allsworth Ross in sociology—both of whom shared much of Ward's ideas

in education; and Van Hise built Wisconsin's extension department into state education's most ambitious effort to place, in
Van Hise's words, "the accumulated knowledge" of man at the
service of the state's citizenry. Convinced, like Ward, that great
social waste resulted from depriving the lower classes of educational opportunity, Van Hise tried to take the facilities of the
university to as many state citizens as its resources would permit.
During the Progressive Era years of Robert La Follette's gov-
ernorship, the university supplied experts in various fields to
solve state problems, to draft model legislation, to mold public
opinion to support public education by appeals to enlightened
self-interest, and to train a generation of dedicated public
servants. Van Hise's practical demonstration of the social reform
potential of state education confirmed the possibilities of Ward's
theoretical position.

But, after fully admitting its merits, Ward's faith in education
still strains modern man's credulity concerning his estimate of
the possible effect of knowledge in meliorating social problems
and his underestimation of the corruptive influence of power
in whatever form it might take. Despite these limitations, Ward's
views were certainly refreshing when compared to the elitest
views of eugenicists and his opponents in established educational
circles. A professional educator and psychologist like Edward L.
Thorndike, for example, held biases that led him to accuse
Ward of "intellectual communism"; Thorndike asserted that it
was much more productive for society to subsidize fifteen
research professorships than to invest the funds in the annual
schooling of fifteen hundred young children.[27] Ward's excesses
were at least those of a man of good hope. His optimism, moreover, that the major evils in society were due not to the nature
of mankind but to the bad management of its opportunities and
development made possible a theoretical ground for social
reform that was absolutely essential to preserve whatever remained of democratic values and social happiness in the
twentieth century.

In assessing the value of Ward's educational theories, it is
apparent that many of his educational values continue to live
in the mainstream of American ideal thought: the desirability
of full educational opportunity to all people regardless of their

birth, an emphasis on the potentialities of each student rather than his limitations, and a preference for environmental rather than inherent constitutional explanations for explaining human development. Yet in these ideas Ward was not unique; nor was he widely influential, as he, himself, acknowledged. Nevertheless, his ideas still live because of continued antipathy to many of the same social evils that infuriated Ward's sense of justice: the exploitation of large numbers of people because of their ignorance or perverted training; the unhappiness and frustration in people's lives because of limited opportunity to develop their talents; and the practice, under whatever guise, of prejudging a person's worth by arbitrary standards of value.

Many of Ward's criticisms of certain contemporary educational practices were and remain valid. Detail and isolated fact too often substitute for significance and meaning as the product of education. Attention to the gifted few is seldom matched with that for the multitude of average ability students. And his interest in insuring that occupational training did not ignore the broader aspects of education was quite needed, as were his warnings against the personal and social dangers of over-specialization.

The systems approach to learning theory has revived interest in information as a major dimension of education, as Ward had insisted, yet his emphasis on the acquisition of knowledge as the core of an educational program appears more mechanistic than desirable and less possible given the knowledge revolution that has grown by geometric proportions in the present century. As children of wealthy families find limited faith in the possession of material goods to satisfy their deepest needs, so the children of informational abundance hold little brief for personal salvation through the accumulation of knowledge. Furthermore, the scientific supports for Ward's educational beliefs based on Locke's pleasure-pain psychology and on Lamarck's theory of inheritance had already lost intellectual respectability before his death; but they were really not needed to justify the desirability of universal public education.

A number of Ward's ideas were certainly vague, verging on empty verbalisms; and his educational works were largely repetitious restatements of a few simple themes. Practically no

effort was made by Ward to gather objective data to test or to
develop his ideas, although his lack of educational research was
due in large part to the breadth of his occupational and avoca-
tional activities. Furthermore, one suspects that Ward's unshak-
able faith in the utility of education to solve society's ills served
as much as a compensatory psychological defense as it did as
a fully conscious solution for the multifactored personal and
social problems of a complex industrial society. Education was
and would continue to be a powerful force; so too would the
basic optimism and hope that permeated Ward's educational
theories. Yet Americans have all too frequently deluded themselves about the magnitude of social reform possible through
education unsupported by other types of structural changes
and human insights. That same faith in Ward, however, clearly
reflects in a remarkable way the spirit of his age; it reminds
Americans that the "Gilded Age," the "age of enterprise," and
the "age of excess" held hope that the spirit of man might
prevail over the sociological and technological ills that he had
created. As Laurence Cremin concludes in his evaluation of
Ward's influence on progressive education, "Ward's work was
marked by a brilliance quite comparable to Spencer's and
Sumner's; and in moving education to the forefront of human
affairs, he gave 'scientific' expression to a theme that had flowed
as part of the American mainstream from Jefferson through Mann
and Harris to the generation of the eighties."[28]

CHAPTER 3

Natural Science

I Optimistic Evolutionist

LESTER Ward earned his principal livelihood for nearly twenty-five years as a natural scientist in one of the most active scientific centers in the country. Yet, despite his avid curiosity in things scientific, Ward's work in his paleobotany specialty, while quite respectable, never produced the scientific reputation or the theoretical breakthroughs that he had confidently expected in his earlier years.[1] But, throughout the scientific controversies of the period, Ward strove to present evolutionary theory in a form that was consistent with the activism and the optimism that characterized his and his society's spirit.

Under Powell's direction of the Geological Survey, Ward was given wide latitude to educate himself in paleobotany and to carry his research wherever it might lead. During the 1880's and 1890's, while quartered on the south balcony of the Smithsonian Museum, Ward engaged in prodigious research and publication. He authored nearly one hundred and fifty paleobotanic articles and about a half dozen exhaustive monographs about the history of paleobotany and about the classification and distribution of fossilized American flora. His personal herbarium of over five thousand plant species became a major element of the Smithsonian's collection. A continuous project, his "Compendium of Paleobotany" was a bibliographic reference which contained at the time he left the survey nearly eighty thousand references to descriptions and illustrations of fossil plants and a bibliography of twelve thousand titles.[2] Ward's devotion to the painstaking work of recording and classifying fossil information reflected his awareness of the need for such

67

an initial informational stage in any new science and his own need to have a complete body of factual information at his fingertips before he ventured into publication with academically trained scientists for whom he continued to feel both deference and apprehension.

Scientific circles in America in the years following the Civil War were caught up in the contagion produced by the concept of organic evolution. Darwin's epic *On the Origin of Species* (1859) stimulated their efforts to test the validity of the conception of natural origins and natural selection in all life forms as well as in social structures. Ward, who first read Darwin in a French translation in 1869, later called his discovery of evolution "a vast psychic earthquake."[3] During the following decade, Ward attempted to reconcile the English biologist's views with those of other European scientists whose work he was reading. His translation of the work of the German evolutionary embryologist, Ernst Haeckel, was among the first English translations available in America.[4] Even more important to Ward's own thought was his movement from Darwin to Herbert Spencer; for Ward, like Spencer, was drawn to extend the evolutionary hypothesis from the organic to the cosmic world. Organic evolution, Ward speculated, was but a minor manifestation of a universal evolution toward the concentration and integration of matter that was followed in time by the reverse force of dissolution. The earth, at present, he concluded in his optimistic rending of cosmic theory, existed in its ascending evolutionary stage of the integration of matter. Humanity, whatever its eventual doom, was still in a process of creation that made progress possible.[5]

From the first, Ward was eager to embrace and to apply Darwin's conclusions. Coinciding with his own rejection of orthodox religion, Darwin's natural evolution promised an authoritative explanation for the natural world and a method to push back farther the veil of ignorance and superstition that Ward believed thwarted people's chance for happiness. Ward's concern with the need to educate the broader public through popularized science influenced much of his science writing. Copies of his early guide to the flora of the Washington, D. C., area, for example, were distributed by him to all the teachers in the local school system; lectures and discussions were given by him and others in the local scientific societies at meetings that were open to the public; and innovative educational techniques, such as the use of paleobotanical lantern slides, were devised to wean people away from superstitious folklore and to lead them to rationalistic explanations for phenomena based on a materialistic understanding of the universe. Ward took time each day at the Smithsonian to append to daily army department weather maps his own weather forecasts and his own meteorological explanations for the edification of the visiting public; his purpose was not only the possible utility of his predictions but, more importantly, the development of public understanding "that the weather was a domain of law and natural causation."[6]

Unfortunately, Ward's professional work in natural science suffered from the common defects of his period. Some of these, such as his penchant to coin neologisms to express his ideas, were true of other scientists who were developing new concepts in new areas. A more serious defect was Ward's proclivity to classify when he might better have speculated and to speculate when he should have experimented. Taxonomy, the systematic classification of organisms, absorbed the greatest share of his time in the Geological Survey. Insistent upon classifying every shred of paleobotanical evidence and of finding every bibliographic entry that pertained to his specimens, Ward's caution led too often to a small vision of paleobotany. As a result, his final natural science activity was the writing of botanical entries for *The Century Dictionary* and for *Webster's International Dictionary*. There was nothing petty in such enterprise and much of it was necessary, if tedious; but his limiting himself to taxonomical issues kept him from exploring newer scientific questions and from questioning the terms of his own systematizing efforts.

The counterpart of Ward's encyclopedic efforts to establish evolutionary sequences in prehistoric plant life was his philosophical speculations on evolutionary theory which, while occasionally insightful, were never supported with experimental documentation which might have attracted the attention of other biologists. As a result, his shrewd observations with scientific potential were either buried in philosophical treatises or abandoned whenever further evidence was demanded.

One reinforcement for the Darwinian theory of evolution that Ward did contribute was his evidence in support of the idea of the incomplete adaptation of many organisms to their environment.[7] Nearly any plant transplanted from its wild condition to one of human cultivation, he observed, thrived more vigorously in its body structure; moreover, plants that were transplanted from one country to another often flourished to such an extent that they drove out indigenous plants. Nature had not provided each species with an environment best suited to its fullest development; nature displayed no teleological intelligence. Rather, each plant had an inherent potential for growth that was limited by its environment to the comparatively imperfect organization with which it was found in nature. Because what an organism presently was did not indicate what it was capable of becoming, the optimistic implication for the human organism was clear.

Thus, Ward's interest in evolutionary theory was tied to his intellectual need to find a consistent, all-embracing scientific principle that could make rational the diversity and the change that he observed in the natural and social worlds around him. Ward, like his upper class counterpart, Henry Adams, belonged to the last generation of American intellectuals who hoped that they could find a monistic scientific law that would explain the nature and destiny of man, as well as unite and make comprehensible the phenomena of geology, biology, and the other sciences. But, unlike Adams, Ward's objective was a hopeful cosmic theory that would support the aspirations of a self-confident, working class society that was upward bound. Religious cosmologies had been rejected by Ward as factually inaccurate and as fatalistic even before he read Darwin, and he contended in *Dynamic Sociology* that, while there was mechanical order in nature, there was no anthropomorphic design.[8]

To view man as a minute element of an infinite universe could lead some men to Nihilism and to understand the inevitable evolution and dissolution of the earth and its inhabitants would lead others to despair. But, for Ward, an evolutionary optimist, an understanding of the magnitude of time and space and of the short duration of man's past, compared with an estimated twenty-five-million-year future, suggested that man had only just begun to exist. "His golden age," he wrote at age sixty-six, "is before him and not behind him." In contrast with the cooling spectacle of Mars, the earth's inhabitants should be inspired by their planet's youthfulness and by the unlimited evolutionary opportunities that lay before them.[9]

II *Neo-Darwinism and Neo-Lamarckianism*

Lester Ward, along with nearly all American biologists and social philosophers in the generation following the Civil War, accepted the idea of biological transmission to their descendants of certain characteristics acquired by organisms during their lifetime. The concept itself was quite old, as an established element in the folk beliefs of Western culture, but early in the nineteenth century it received a scientific formulation and the name of its formulator—Chevalier de Lamarck, a French naturalist. Lamarck held that the habitual exercise of an organ by any creature increased the capacity of the organ and that any structural modifications were preserved thereafter through biological inheritance. Darwin, as well as most early Darwinians, accepted Lamarckianism as one source of the variation in species which provided the occasion for the operation of natural selection. The young Ward, like other early supporters of evolutionary theory, was happy to accept theoretical support wherever it might be found; and, given the very real inadequacies in Darwinian theory to explain the origin of variations, he too brought Lamarck into service. In Ward's case, the acceptance of Lamarck by Comte and Spencer, his key intellectual mentors, served to confirm his acceptance of the idea.

Just as important to Ward as the biological necessity of Lamarckianism to explain the origin of variability was its sociological utility. American reformers, because of the very history of their society and its ethos, were drawn to environmental and institutional programs of reform as those most consistent with American values and aspirations. Lamarckianism provided a source of legitimacy in validating the efficacy of social reform; the improvements of one generation could be passed on, like its sins, to subsequent generations. From this foundation, it was possible to affirm a belief in unilinear progress for American society and to create the public opinion necessary to provide the financial and political support needed by most reform movements.[10]

Lamarckianism, like other early scientific concepts based on shrewd guesses and philosophical conclusions, was shy of experimental confirmation. In fact, it was particularly vulnerable to association with crude tales of the inheritance of mutilations and marks on the offspring of women traumatized during pregnancy. In the late 1880's, evolutionary scientists and social reformers who rested their premises on biological evolution were forced to reconsider their Lamarckian assumptions because of the experimental evidence offered by a German embryologist at the University of Freiburg, August Weismann, whose studies, conducted during the 1880's and first published in English in 1889, sought to demonstrate that, because of the nature of cellular action at the heart of the reproduction process, only germ—or sex—cells were involved; there was no way for the more ordinary body—or somatic—cells to influence the hereditarian transmission carried by the germ plasm. Acquired characteristics gained through exercise or from the effect of environment could not be passed on to progeny; an organism could inherit only those traits provided by the germ cells of its parents. Natural selection alone, concluded Weismann, which operated on the variations created by the complex union of ancestral germ plasms from dual parents and by less-well-explained genetic "sports," or mutations, explained the processes of biological evolution.

Lester Ward, confronted with Weismann's challenge to his understanding of biological evolution and evolutionary social reform, as well as faced with the necessity of preparing a presidential address for the Biological Society of Washington, spent the summer of 1890 bouncing in a buckboard over the Triassic terrain of Maryland and Virginia reading Weismann and drafting his response. When his address "Neo-Darwinism and Neo-Lamarckism" finally emerged, it was a vigorous criticism of Weismann's "hypotheses" and a reaffirmation of the "laws" of

Neo-Lamarckianism.[11] The warmth of Ward's reply suggests that in the absence of a concept of culture that was severed from all biological connections, to abandon Lamarck while accepting Weismann was, to Ward, an abandonment of the social sciences to unrestrained biological determinism.[12] The difficulty for Ward in parting company with Lamarck was the absence of an alternative theory of culture with scientific authority that could legitimize the efficacy of social reform activity. Before Weismann, it had been possible in Lamarckianism to emphasize the cultural aspect of a mixed sociobiological process, but to Ward it now seemed necessary to choose between race and culture. The nature of cultural change had not yet been severed from the biological processes that found shelter in the muddied biocultural terminology of Lamarckianism.

Ward's lecture to the Washington area biologists in early 1891 initiated his spirited campaign to maintain room for Lamarckianism in evolutionary theory. During the campaign, however, Ward conceded increasing territory to the Neo-Darwinians. The contest continued into the 1900's for Ward, as it did for many other American social scientists; but the evidence in his work suggests that he reluctantly gave up Lamarck as the weight of contrary evidence accumulated and as he recognized more hostile deterministic forces in the eugenics movement. Yet the importance of Lamarck to Ward's social thought makes "social Lamarckianism" as accurate a description of his thinking as does the more commonly ascribed designation of "social Darwinism."

Ward based his defense of Lamarckianism on two main grounds: the failure of Weismann to provide a satisfactory explanation of the appearance of variations and the very limited knowledge yet confirmed about the very minute and largely unknown processes of heredity. The verdict was not yet in, he contended; and, until it was, Lamarck's reliability should be presumed because of the assistance his ideas had provided Darwin and because of the pragmatic value they retained for influencing public support of social action. Ward did not spare Lamarck in his critique, however. The French naturalist had not recognized the operation of natural selection, and Ward never doubted that that process was much more instrumental in the course of evolution than Lamarck's "law of exercise" was. Many of the examples of variation credited to acquired characteristics, he admitted, were no doubt less clearly understood actions of natural selection. And the tendency of Lamarck and later proponents to believe that accidental mutilations could be transmitted to offspring was disavowed by Ward, although he accused the Neo-Darwinians of continuing their fire on such straw men.

In Weismann's work, Ward was particularly critical of how the embryologist could explain hereditary variation if environment could not cause specific changes and if the substance of germ plasm could only be explained by referring it back to more ancestral germ plasm. From whence, Ward questioned, could the ancestral variations have appeared? Both Weismann and Ward at this stage minimized mutations, but Ward was later able to accept mutations as a substantial replacement for acquired characteristics since his ego found consolation in his earlier "fortuitous variation" theory of heredity that came close to the concept of mutations.[13]

The transmission of heredity, Ward conceded, was a subtle process not yet fully understood. He was unable to supply evidence to support his modified Lamarckian beliefs; but, he insisted, neither was Weismann able to demonstrate empirically the source of variation. "The truth is," he suggested at one point, "that the real phenomena of heredity are too recondite for direct observation."[14] Nevertheless, he defensively argued that the burden of proof rested on the embryologists; and, until proof was supplied, the idea of the inheritance of acquired characteristics should be accepted because of its pragmatic utility.

By utility, Ward, of course, referred to the effect that scientific ideas might have on human behavior. The importance of Ward's automatic intellectual reflex to draw the social implications from a debate on the nature of biological evolution became clear in the concluding remarks of his Washington address and in his later amplification of those ideas in an article for laymen.[15] Unfortunately, the urge to judge his scientific ideas by a test of their pragmatic value to society locked Ward in to his Lamarckian position. What most exasperated him about Weismann, he admitted, was the contention that environment could affect germ plasm in only an irrational haphazard fashion, while application, effort, and the habits of the organism were of no account. "If nothing that the individual gains by the most heroic or the most assiduous effort can by any possibility be handed on to posterity," he wrote, "the incentive to effort is in great part removed. If all the labor bestowed upon the youth of the race to secure a perfect physical and intellectual development dies with the individual to whom it is imparted, why this labor?"[16] In short, Weismannism was a socially immoral and un-American ethic.

What Ward feared was that Weismann's conclusions would bolster the proponents of laissez faire and of social determinism. If effort and social reform could not change man, then it was absurd to try either one. The public's tenuous financial support to education was particularly in jeopardy, he believed, by this new refinement in "nature-worship." Consequently, it was to the effects on education of the debate between the neo-Lamarckians and the neo-Darwinians that he devoted his popular writing on heredity.[17] While most mental traits were non-advantageous in the struggle for survival, he contended that those of cunning, money getting, and political intrigue had held survival value as had the competitive traits in lower animals. But the higher intellectual and ethical faculties, he maintained, had not been advantageous in a competitive jungle and could only have survived through other than natural selection processes. The growth of capacity, which he assumed in those traits, could only have been created by the incremental increases of each generation that exercised its brain cells and that transmitted the structural increase to its progeny.

The neo-Lamarckians, he stressed, had never believed that knowledge or culture was transmitted directly to descendants through heredity. Only the *capacity* for acquiring knowledge was hereditary. Each generation had to acquire anew the knowledge that humanity had accumulated and that other or following generations had inherited—a sufficiently discouraging circumstance in itself. Yet the social need was imperative; each generation had to replenish and exercise the store of knowledge or else both the social inheritance of the knowledge content and the biological inheritance of cellular capacity would diminish. The struggle had always been uphill, he suggested, so the "comforting popular belief" in the transmission of acquired characteristics had emerged to bolster the morale of those in that struggle. While this pragmatic explanation for the origin of the idea suggests that Ward was less than sure of the scientific accuracy of Lamarckianism itself, he feared any immediate acceptance of Weismann would dangerously weaken the public's resolve to support the education and the social ethic of work on which he believed civilization depended. So, he concluded, "until the doctors of science shall cease to differ on this point and shall reduce the laws of heredity to a degree of exactness which shall amount to something more like a demonstration than the current speculations, it may perhaps be as well to continue for a time to hug the delusion."[18]

Ward continued the neo-Lamarckian debate until the mid-1890's, but in substance he conceded territory to Weismann at the same time that he proclaimed Weismann's concessions.[19] After Weismann was willing to accept the influence of climate and nutrition on the germ plasm, Ward was apparently satisfied that environment as an important biological and social force was preserved as a weapon against the naturalistic determinists; and he edged out of the debate. Lamarckianism had become the symbol for environmentalism; but, when the broader environmental principle had been accepted in however muted a fashion, Ward was willing—though reluctantly—to abandon his espousal of the inheritance of acquired characteristics.[20]

By the time *Applied Sociology* was published in 1906, Ward no longer mentioned the inheritance of acquired characteristics, credited himself with supplying new information to Weismann, and placed himself in full accord with the matured neo-Darwinian position in his brief discussion of genetic inheritance. "This view," he now found, despite a lingering trace of Lamarck, "has its hopeful or optimistic side, for, as we have seen, nothing is ever wholly lost, and the accumulations of unnumbered generations continue to exist, ... ultimately to come forth and exert their due influence upon the world."[21]

III *Eugenics*

The scientific issue that most concerned Lester Ward during the last decade of his life was the heightened interest in eugenics as a scientific program for social reform. Eugenics, the science of improved human genetic engineering, was directly tied to the earlier controversy between the Neo-Darwinians and the Neo-Lamarckians. As the evidence began to accumulate after 1900 that supported Weismann's position that acquired characteristics could not be inherited, interest in eugenics as a scientific method of human progress increased. The discovery of the work of the Austrian monk, Gregor Mendel, whose studies about the laws of inheritance had been derived from the experimental breeding of peas, provided fresh evidence and a method of study to refine the work begun by Weismann to determine how inheritance actually functioned. While older biologists and many biosocial reformers held tenaciously to the Lamarckian assumptions, most spokesmen with recognized scientific credentials were forced by 1905 to 1910 to accept the probable validity of Weismann's conclusions.

What the new understanding of inheritance and genetics meant for social reformers interested in science was the necessity for their creating either a new reform program or a new rationale stripped of the Lamarckian assurances in older programs. The problem, of course, was that most social reform in nineteenth-century America had been based on environmental or institutional underpinnings. Such a position was quite tenable when scientists and lay spokesmen alike believed that human improvements in one generation were passed on incrementally to the next through biological inheritance. But, if the nexus connecting social reform with biological reform was nonexistent, then environmental reforms were of more limited utility than had been assumed.

Eugenicists proposed to work through biological methods of human improvement that were consistent with Weismann's findings on germ plasm and with the behavior of those discrete units of heredity control that Mendel's work suggested. Accordingly, American eugenics leaders saw their movement as "the science of the improvement of the human race by better breeding."[22]

Dividing their objectives into negative eugenics (the prohibition of the mating of people with poor genetic endowments and the sterilization of the mentally and morally unfit) and positive eugenics (social and legal encouragement, especially through financial subsidies, for the procreation of children by genetically well-endowed parents) the eugenicists moved into one of the many positions in the Progressive Era's reform spectrum.[23] Eugenicists were among the new liberals when it came to an expansion of political power into areas of individual prerogatives, but they were fundamentally conservative when measured by the criteria of class, race, and style of life that were deemed desirable for future genetic engineering.

In America, the various expressions of eugenic thought were based between the 1870's and 1905 largely on some of the implications of Darwin's theories as they were most clearly interpreted by the British scientist Francis Galton. The reputation of Galton and the university and voluntary association support given him encouraged a small number of American biologists, officers of institutions for the insane and feebleminded, and old-stock aristocrats, fearful of the birthrates of new ethnic groups, to organize a parallel American eugenic reform movement. In 1903, agricultural breeders and university biologists formed an American Breeders' Association. In 1906 a committee on eugenics within the association was created which included such prominent members as David Starr Jordan, biologist and first president and chancellor of Stanford University; Alexander Graham Bell; Charles R. Henderson, a University of Chicago sociologist; and Charles Benedict Davenport, a biology instructor at Harvard University and at the University of Chicago.

Davenport, impressed with the work of Galton and fearful of genetic deterioration in America, persuaded the Carnegie Institution of Washington, an early philanthropic foundation, to underwrite in 1904 a station for experimental evolution at Cold Spring Harbor on Long Island with himself as director. By 1910, Davenport obtained private funding for a eugenics record office at Cold Spring Harbor; and, from that point, the eugenics movement, with Davenport as its chief propagandist, became a minor force in American reform. Social reform was futile, Davenport and other eugenicists contended, since it did not deal with what they believed was the fundamental genetic causation of behavioral problems. Through research in human genetics, the compilation of family genetic records, the encouragement of voluntary genetic counselling before marriage, and the support of legislation that would sterilize "defectives," they mobilized a particular interpretation of Weismann's and Mendel's ideas on heredity into a reform program.

Ward, along with other Darwinians, had long before recognized the possibility of human control of natural selection as one method to increase man's capacity for progress. In an article in the mid-1880's in which Ward briefly commented on Galton's work, he agreed that, if heredity was to be the only mechanism for social improvement, then the systematic propagation of humans, as successfully applied to plants and animals, was a program that promised practical results. Such a program, he argued, however, was unnecessary since "the germs of some form of talent exist in a latent state in nearly every undeveloped intellect, and may be brought out by opportunity."[24] Arguing by analogy from his experience with plants, Ward held that the problem of human development was not one of capacity but of cultivation; consequently, Galton's proposals were less practical than making the environment more favorable to the development of human faculties.

While Galton's eugenic ideas remained in the air during the 1890's, few Americans, including Ward, gave them much notice. With the increased attention and authority given to the power of germ cells that followed the Mendelian breakthrough and the gradual acceptance of Weismann's ideas, Ward became aware of the revived interest in eugenic reform. In a number of book reviews, he began to criticize scientific and social writers who were so carried away with the idea of physiological and genetic degeneracy "that they lose all sense of perspective and become wholly pessimistic."[25] Much of *Applied Sociology*, published in 1906, was an effort to counter the arguments of Galton, Cesare Lombroso, and other proponents of the biological ir- irrepressibility of genius and degeneracy.[26]

To help restore the perspective of public opinion in the matter, and by so doing to galvanize support for environmental reforms, Ward dusted off some old lectures and wrote a long

essay for the syndicated press. Published simultaneously in nine
of the largest urban dailies on the Sunday before Christmas
in 1907, Ward's article attacked once again the hereditarian
school and the idea that talent was genetically limited in the
American population.[27] Genius lay latent throughout society,
Ward insisted; and, no matter what the genetic endowment,
a favorable environment was essential for any talent to emerge.
The environment to which he referred was not so much physical
nature as it was the social environment. When it was propitious,
he asserted, the potential genius blossomed; "even the race to
which he belongs, the current belief to the contrary notwith-
standing, has been found to be an almost negligible factor
whenever a thorough test has been applied."[28] Ward evidently
had in mind the French study by Alfred Odin that he had
reproduced in *Applied Sociology* since none of the eugenic
statistical studies, as he noted, nor many of the American
sociological studies, infected as they were by white racism,
bore out his contention.

Until the last months of Ward's life, he hammered away at
the eugenicists. In a lecture delivered before the Federation for
Child Study in New York, less than three months before his
death, the septuagenarian declared that the hereditarians who
had preceded him to the podium were the new embodiment of
an "oligocentric world view which . . . would center the entire
attention of the world upon an almost infinitesimal fraction of
the human race and ignore all the rest."[29] Such centering of
attention upon the gifted few and such seeking to expand the
incidence of their germ plasm were obnoxious to Ward. "I want
a field that shall be broad enough to embrace the whole human
race," he proclaimed.[30]

The idea of selecting superior people for exclusive or accelerated reproduction Ward found quite unacceptable. The
problem, he pointed out, was in deciding *who* should be given
the power to select criteria and to determine which people
would be allowed to reproduce. In ancient times, absolute
monarchs controlled the food and clothing of their subjects.
But the most sumptuary decrees of feudal days would be liberty
itself compared to any attempts by society to control the choice
of partners in marital relationships. "This," said Ward, "would

be a tyranny by the side of which all other tyrannies would fade into insignificance."[31]

If the eugenicists attempted only to encourage, rather than to enforce, preferred pairings, Ward forecast, they would be unable to overcome the enormous force of human passion. Remembering, no doubt, his tempestuous courtships of Lizzie and Rose, he opined that two persons emotionally attracted to each other would not stop to inquire whether they were fitted to carry on the standard or to improve the quality of the species. Any people who did stop to consider their genetic endowments would probably conclude that no deficiencies existed, and so the very few cases in which any changes in conjugation occurred would produce no appreciable effect upon either society or the race. The effort of the upper classes to establish "social and artificial restraints" was more likely to bring about biological degeneracy and social decadence than any reproductive consideration among the lower classes. Eugenicists, representing the upper classes, ignored their own frustration of nature's methods while casting all the onus on the lower classes.

In part, Ward contended, the eugenicists were misled by mistaken emphases. In the first instance, he argued, the eugenicists placed undue emphasis upon intellectual qualities to the exclusion of all others. Following Galton's lead, their attention focused on producing hereditary genius through improvement of the brain. If their efforts were ever successful, Ward exaggerated, the human head would become so enlarged that natural birth would become impossible. "Like the breeders of cattle, they would 'breed for points,' and the head is the only organ that they seek to develop."[32] In emphasizing brain power, the eugenicists ignored the emotional side of man's being. Nature showed greater wisdom, Ward claimed, by seeking to develop all faculties and to avoid all extremes. A perfect race would be developed in all human qualities—physical, moral, and intellectual; and it was not clear that eugenicists could, even if they were interested, affect all these behavioral traits through biological means.

Second, Ward charged, the eugenicists placed undue emphasis upon the illborn. To read their literature, he remarked, one would conclude that the majority of mankind was defective.

Citing census report statistics to the contrary, Ward pointed out that defectives numbered less than one-half percent of the population. Criticizing graphs and diagrams drawn by Galton and others that exaggerated the presence of overt geniuses and defectives alike, Ward argued, in what was perhaps the most optimistic assertion in all his writing, that of the 99.4 percent of the normal population base, at least fifty percent contained latent genius and talent scattered "somewhat uniformly" through the whole population. Under these circumstances, it was not a breeding program for more brains that was called for, but rather a program to insure opportunity and knowledge for the classes and races that had not yet been stimulated.

Shifting his argument, Ward charged that a number of the popularizers of eugenics, including former President Theodore Roosevelt and his sociologist friend Edward A. Ross, sought to arouse support for the hereditarians by raising the specter of "race suicide." Their contention was, Ward repeated, that the better—or upper—classes were failing to reproduce themselves while the poorer—or immigrant and lower—classes were creating the population growth. Ward attacked the implied assumptions in the "race suicide" thesis. The reason for the birthrate decline among the upper classes was not due to selfishness or fear of the lower classes, Ward asserted; rather, it was due to intelligence and the improved environment of their life. For these people, it was no longer necessary to have numerous children in order to insure the continuation of the species. Through education, moreover, they were sufficiently enlightened to refuse to furnish soldiers to gratify the ambitions of militaristic governments. Since they preferred quality to quantity, they were accomplishing the feat through the humane method of birth control restraints and through the enlightenment of their children.

In regard to the other assumption in the "race suicide" case for eugenics, Ward refused to accept the idea that the upper classes monopolized genetic quality, as they did wealth, or that the contrary was true of the lower classes. Economic condition did not reflect physical or mental potential. The hampered poor, though ill-bred, were wellborn; and, by infusing new and varied hereditary lines into the American population, the poor constituted "the hope of society": "Those swarming, spawning millions, the bottom layer of society, the proletariat, the working classes, the 'hewers of wood and drawers of water,' nay, even the denizens of the slums—that all these are by nature the peers of the boasted 'aristocracy of brains' that now dominates society and looks down upon them, and the equals in all but privilege of the most enlightened teachers of eugenics."[33] Ward's scientific evidence was scanty, but his insight into the social perversion of scientific ideas was acute. He could not have wished for a valedictory more in keeping with his optimistic affirmation of the American democratic faith.

CHAPTER 4

Search for an Applied Science of Government

I *Environmental Influences on an Environmental Theory*

LESTER Ward's political motivations and specific political ideas are closely related to his social and intellectual experience. The deep impression of rural poverty, religious idealism, and family pride in ability and workmanship combined to create in all of the Ward brothers a lively interest in political reform. When high ambitions instilled by parents and a democratic social ethos were thwarted by a seemingly inequitable reward structure during periods of highly visible economic growth, the result was a family of articulate reformers. Cyrenus Ward, for example, Lester's brother who manufactured wagon hubs in Pennsylvania, turned from bankruptcy to study the causes of the nation's economic cycles and the plight of worker-capitalists like himself.

The drive for success, respectability, and academic accomplishment that was so common to the Wards led Cyrenus to New York where he became a spokesman for the fledgling Socialist movement. In 1878, Cyrenus published *A Labor Catechism of Political Economy* which detailed his arguments for state control of industry.[1] From 1880 to 1884, Cyrenus published *The Voice of the People*, a Socialist newspaper, in New York. When he exhausted his funds in 1884, Lester found him a minor post in the Bureau of Labor where he wrote his two volume major work, *The Ancient Lowly*. The first volume, *History of the Ancient Working People* (1889), details various labor uprisings and cooperative movements in ancient Greece and Rome.[2] His even longer second volume, *The Origins of Socialism*, published in 1900, was more Marxian than the first volume; but it contains a curiously strong religious tone.[3]

This same drive of the Ward brothers for public recognition, literary accomplishment, collective endeavor, and democratic politics is also found in Lorenzo Ward, the oldest of the brothers, who was left the family farm in Iowa. As one of Lorenzo's sons wrote Lester upon the death of his father, Lorenzo was "always of an uneasy mind, no sooner out of one thing than he would rush head long into another." The richness of his Iowa land and the hard work of his family paid off various mortgages incurred in his efforts "to really succeed."[4] In his seventy-fifth year, Lorenzo bought a half interest in a Populist newspaper in Iowa and became its editor; and, since prosperity had finally given him a pulpit, he preached "Labor for the Laborless, Money for the Moneyless, Homes for the Homeless." Prohibition, public education, and "attractive laws" by a strong national government were the editorial objectives of *The Farmers Alliance*.[5]

For Lester, the youngest of the brothers, an interest in political affairs emerged early, as indicated by his diary accounts. The young Ward eagerly supported Abolition and the election of Abraham Lincoln in 1860; slavery, alcohol, and Southern secessionist views, he wrote, should be destroyed by the power of the central government.[6] The successful conclusion of the Civil War confirmed the views that young Ward had already taken: the power of mobilized government to work good in society, the need for government activity on a national scope, and the availability of people from all classes to join in a common undertaking to achieve the goals of society.

Ward's permanent residence in Washington, D. C., after the war, with an occupation tied directly to the activity of the national government, and his later government-sponsored expeditions to the farthest reaches of the nation, made a national political science axiomatic to Ward's reform-oriented mind. Above all else, his employment for twenty-five years in the Geological Survey among practical but idealistic scientists prompted his confidence in the dawning of a government administered on a scientific basis. Clearly, his reputation and his economic security, as well as his ideals, would be advanced by the growth of a professional, administrative bureaucracy at the expense of the legislature with its arbitrary and fluctuating policies and budgets.

II *Political Theory*

The foundation of Lester Ward's political thought was rooted in his asumption that man had the intellectual ability to overcome the strongest kinds of physical and social environmental obstacles.[7] Many men, joining their abilities and powers in a common cause through political organization, had even greater opportunity to control environment for their own purposes. Neither humanity in general, nor a poor boy from the Midwest, was a helpless pawn of economic, religious, or psychological forces. The American success mythology wedded to optimistic evolutionary science gave birth to a new democratic theory of government that repudiated both laissez-faire Individualism and Marxian Socialism.

Underlying Ward's political theory were certain philosophical premises. The first of these was that the universe in its natural and human dimensions could be understood by the mind of man. Through scientific processes, the order inherent within nature and human behavior could be formulated into law; by being known, it could be used by man for his own ends. As a physical scientist and a philosophical monist, Ward confidently assumed that similar types of order existed in social, as well as natural, spheres and that scientific methods devised for the natural sciences could be applied to the social life of man. The political activity of man, therefore, could be studied with the assurance that reliable generalizations could be made.

Ward held that an analysis of static politics was a "pure" science that was unbiased, outside of partisan involvement, and disinterested in change. Pure science was that which did not attempt to promote purposeful activity; it only sought to describe it. Beyond that level of examination lay "applied" science with a dynamic analysis that, by its predictive capabilities, could formulate and implement progressive social change through political mechanisms. "We must not be content with the actual," Ward wrote; "we must imagine the possible and strive to attain it."[8] Nonetheless, his years spent as an insecure federal bureaucrat taught him to take to the high ground in any discussion that might invoke partisan emotions among the elected officials who controlled the bureaucracy.

Ward always claimed that he was a social scientist with no interest in politics itself. A practicing politician was an artist, he held, not a scientist. The social scientist had no quarrel with any political party or movement; he observed them all as data for his disinterested observations. Ward's claim to political neutrality was rather humorous since he was very much interested in particular issues; and, while less partisan between the Republicans and Democrats in 1900 than he had been in 1865, he always made sure his "scientific" judgments were on the side of that party or movement that promoted an institutional network of trained intelligence to control the course of national development. Ward was above politics, but only to the extent that he would be in a better position to influence whoever might be in office.

A second premise underlying Ward's political theory was the concept of social lag. According to Ward, the conservative tendencies of society often perpetuated customs and ideas after they had lost whatever earlier value they had once had. Social theories became, therefore, as antiquated as preindustrial technology. Any science of politics, he believed, symptomatic of later pragmatic theory, would consequently have to examine all political ideas and practices to see if they were still useful to man, or as useful under new circumstances as alternate ideas would be. Science, then, was his tool to develop new concepts and to validate the value judgments inherent in them.

Ward's political theory drew heavily on French, British, and American Enlightenment figures. The primacy of reason, the reality of natural law, and the social compact origin of government were further premises accepted by Ward with whatever new scientific evidence supported those earlier conclusions. The cautious realism of American Enlightenment theorists was also called upon by Ward. The mechanics of government, as well as general political theory must be created, he urged, upon the real motives and forces that actuate social behavior—not upon what one would like them to be. A science of government should follow where men and society really lived; for "nothing short

of stern objective realities can constitute a safe foundation for
any future moral or social system."[9]

As a student of the Enlightenment, Ward gravitated to a
utilitarian ethic to guide his political thought. What was good
in political ideas and practices was that which was useful, and
what was useful was that which brought the greatest happiness
to the greatest number of people. Man was presently going
through a major historical watershed, Ward proposed, from a
life of pain to a life of potential pleasure. Since nearly all social
and political theory of the past had been based on the pessimistic
stage of pain, new theory would have to be based on pleasure
as the mainspring of social and political life. The future task
of government, he proclaimed, was no less than "the organization
of human happiness."[10]

In order to achieve the utilitarian ethic, Ward reasoned, the
government had to seek the means of increasing social happiness. A science of society was necessary to determine what
produced happiness and how the agencies of happiness could
be stimulated and reinforced by purposeful human activity. It
was at this point when a science of government became "applied," that, in Ward's phrase, "social telesis" occurred.[11] Accordingly, political theory was largely ethical; and a science
of government became a vehicle for the moral progress of
society.

Ward was led to an application of Darwinian evolution to
politics by the writings of Herbert Spencer. Spencer in the
1870's and 1880's became a major force in American intellectual
life, comparable to John Locke a century earlier. While Ward
was stimulated by Spencer's free-wheeling effort to create a
political theory based on evolutionary doctrine, he disagreed
sharply with the conclusions reached by Spencer and echoed
by his laissez-faire disciples in America.

Spencer, like Ward, was a Comtean positivist, convinced that
science could be applied to the study of society. And, like Ward
in another respect, Spencer sought scientific data to justify a
moral philosophy founded quite apart from his scientific studies.
Spencer held that society evolved like an organism in nature
and could be analyzed in terms similar to the biological world.
The laws of evolution which shaped organisms and society

were so deep-seated and pervasive that man could attempt to interject himself into their flow only at his own peril. Since society evolved in a progressive fashion, social evils currently existed which would not remain in the distant future when society became more thoroughly integrated and coherent. But, Spencer claimed, man must rely on the natural evolutionary forces since only they were sufficiently powerful for the long periods necessary to change man's nature.

Ward parted company with Spencer and his principal American disciple William Graham Sumner, social science professor at Yale, over the ascription to human society of the characteristics of a biological organism and the alleged similarity of forces in natural evolution with those in social evolution.[12] Ward insisted that society was not subject to the same developments and life cycles as were organisms; nor, more importantly, was society blindly subject to the slow, uneconomical evolutionary forces that were operative on subrational life forms. The economy of nature that required the Doris sea slug to deposit six hundred thousand eggs to reproduce herself was no guide for man to follow. Nor, he pointed out, was human labor "natural" in the sense Spencer admired, since all labor was an artificial transformation of environment. Whenever Spencer's revered principle of competition was removed in nature, as in the human cultivation of plants, the protected forms grew more luxuriant and varied. The conclusion Ward drew from the scientific evidence about "natural" competition was that it was not only wasteful but prevented the maximum development of a species. All human institutions and cooperative agencies were means of checking "natural" competition, just as the richest corporations cooperated with one another while their poorest and least intelligent employees engaged in rugged competition with their fellows.[13]

Economic reforms through political means were quite proper, Ward argued, and were even within the traditional function of government protection for individuals. Tragically, government still viewed antisocial acts as only individual in nature. "The underpaid labor, the prolonged and groveling drudgery, the wasted strength, the misery and squalor, the disease resulting, and the premature deaths that would be prevented by a just distribution of the products of labor," admonished Ward, "would in a single year outweigh all the so-called crime of a century."[14] It was illogical to forbid aggrandizement by physical force but to allow it by legal fiction. Yet now, Ward noted, social spokesmen like Spencer and Sumner told people to let nature take its course, even though people had not done so in thousands of years. The laws of nature that Spencer endorsed were violated every time a highway robber was arrested and sent to jail. Even the logic of the Spencerians destroyed their position since reformers were the natural product of their environment and consequently were "legitimate" according to natural evolution theories. Reformers, Ward joked, could shout "laissez faire" at those who attacked them.[15]

Ward's assumptions were the basis for a political theory of hope in contrast to the policies of despair that he feared were resulting from scientific determinism in the hands of Spencer, Sumner, Brooks Adams, and Henry Adams. "The very law of evolution threatens to destroy hope and paralyze effort. Science applied to man becomes a gospel of inaction...."[16] He believed his own formulation of the political implications of Darwinian evolution would restore the "gospel of action"—a secularized ethic of work and democratic hope that had crystallized in the early-nineteenth-century success mythology. His own life, he held, based as it was on such a belief, validated his faith. Cast in scientific terminology, the long course of human evolution provided man with a highly developed brain whose mental activity allowed him to escape the genetic evolution of other living organisms and to move to a unique plane of development. In this doctrine, Ward appealed to an ultimate natural law authority that easily rivaled the divine assurance of pre-Civil War religious perfectionists.

On the basis of Ward's belief in the capacity of the human mind, he proceeded to construct a theory of political action and to explain the proper role of government in a scientific age. In his formulation, Ward brought together the Jeffersonian tradition of faith in human potential and the importance of environment, with the Hamiltonian tradition of big government intervention in society to promote the welfare of the nation. The determining power of environment in Ward's theory could justify liberal political reformers as well as conservative apologists for the status quo or pessimistic theorists of extreme environmentalism.

Man's impulse to control found realization in government. While that impulse had often led to cruel and arbitrary government, Ward acknowledged, the government, under conditions of democratic organization and scientific education, could serve society by bringing natural and social conditions under control. The bureaucracy within the executive branch of American government, for example, could become sufficiently educated and professionalized to manage basic social concerns. In an unpublished manuscript of the 1880's, Ward compiled a political agenda for liberal reformers for years to come: quality controls on food products; investigation of the causes and cures of disease; government aid to science, education, hospitals, mental asylums, and archaeological research; public regulation of communications, transportation, utilities, insurance, and banking; and protection from natural disaster.[17] These interests were not isolated individual problems, but the concerns of all members of society. By meliorating them, and others still not yet conceptualized, the government would become the agent for additional social progress.

No government, Ward claimed had yet reached a stage of development where it fulfilled its potential for improving human happiness. Government was still a primitive art instead of a sophisticated science. In a parody of Spencer's organismic analogy of government as the social organism's brain, Ward joked that "the brain of society" had scarcely reached adolescence.[18] Society, and certainly its scientific members, should not rest content with the status quo. Government, he insisted, was a positive institution and could no longer perform only negative actions of repression: "The day has come for society to take its affairs into its own hands and shape its own destinies."[19]

Democratic government, Ward believed, was the most successful form of government to date; the evolutionary tendency, he believed, was in the direction of popular representation that resulted when increased education enabled people to understand better their own interests. Democratic government represented the whole of society, not just a single class. In a democracy, the will of the people was directed toward securing

human happiness; and, since the government held power only
with the approval of the populace, it was motivated to achieve
the maximum social happiness its intelligence and organization
could deliver. Unfortunately, most democratic governments had
underachieved since their officials reflected only the limited
intellectual development of the broader society. Yet even dull-
ness joined with benevolence was better than brilliance joined
with rapacity, as in the case of autocracies. What was clearly
needed was, first of all, a rapid levelling upward of popular
education and intelligence. Second, government should seek to
duplicate in other areas what scientifically trained professional
bureaucrats had achieved in isolated bureaus such as the Department of Agriculture and the Geological Survey.

Ward's own political concerns were less with the specific
policies or structures of governments—although he was always
critical of the House of Representatives—than with the broader
aims of government. The significance of most political events
was greatly overestimated, he reasoned. In most political con-
tests, the opposing forces were so evenly balanced or so similar
that the triumph of either side made little difference to the
sum total of human happiness or to the progress of the race.
The history written about such political activity was only "a
polite amusement"; human progress depended on deeper laws.[20]

Most laws, in a limited government state, were not wrong in
their penal and prohibitive nature; but they were so limited
with an essentially negative conception of government that they
continued to minimize personal liberty. Law should be positive,
Ward insisted. It should harness the energies of men and
society "instead of continually damming the stream of human
desire . . . until it finally bursts over all its barriers and whelms
everything in the ruin of political revolution. . . ."[21] As long as
most laws were mandatory and prohibitive, he said, society
would administer justice little different from irrational creatures
in nature.

What was needed, Ward maintained, was "attractive" legislation that would persuade people to follow it for their own
self-happiness rather than from their fear of punishment. Pre-
sumably, an educational program by the state would enlighten
the individual sufficiently to identify his individual interests with

those of society. Attractive legislation would utilize the natural social forces of man's passions to accomplish society's objectives. Brute power, as in standing armies and militias, would become unnecessary as the government moved to indirect methods; and civil liberty could increase as a result. The quality of legislatures would likewise improve as each true legislator became an applied sociologist and as every legislature became a polytechnic laboratory of research into the theory and practice of "social physics." In fact, Ward suggested, legislators would increasingly view themselves as professional bureaucrats did—as public servants who performed services for the nation. They would abandon their earlier autonomy, work more closely with the administrative branch of government, and by their votes put the sanction of society on decisions already carefully worked out in sociological laboratories.[22]

Ward's democratic political theory expanded the common view of the aims of government into a broad and positive formulation designed to meet the goal of happiness that underlay his ethical system. A government which promoted the well-being of its citizens by means of positive, far-reaching measures, he called a "sociocracy." Ward never advocated anything short of maximum fulfillment and pleasure for individuals; and, accordingly, his theory of government was broad and ambitious.

III *Sociocracy Versus Spencer And Marx*

Ward's conception of a "sociocracy" was built on his faith in the ability of the state to increase individual and social happiness by telic, or purposeful, direction of the social structure. The best methods were indirect, through education, which proceeded more quickly than the Spencerian evolutionary determinists were willing to admit, but more gradually than the Socialists were likely to accept. A sociocracy, wrote Ward, was not dependent on nature to act; it could move to organize human effort and scientific understanding in pursuit of human happiness. Such telic action, displayed on an individual level by Ward's own life, implied no blind optimism. Any passive attitude, wrote Ward, was "suicidal"; the logic of science was action.[23]

Democratic governments of action were being seriously challenged, Ward charged, by "physiocratic" and "plutocratic" alternatives. By a "physiocracy," Ward referred to the type of government advocated by the Physiocrats—Adam Smith, and, more recently, Herbert Spencer. Their laissez-faire ideas, he claimed, were doctrines of despair leading society to inaction. By "plutocracy," Ward meant an organized economic elite that exploited the democratic system in its private interests and did not serve the needs of the broader population. Plutocracy represented "undergovernment"—the failure of government to keep up with the new human needs of an industrial environment. Such "modern brigandage" thrived under weak government, wrote Ward; and, whenever possible, it attempted to influence public opinion to fear strong government. For practical purposes, there was little difference between the results of physiocratic democracy and plutocratic democracy. In either case, people became the victims of industrial unemployment, exploitive wages, monotonous labor, and misery. The counterpart to this exploitation was the luxury and power of the plutocratic few. Yet under weak government, no one saw any alternative to the new types of ills from which society needed protection.[24]

A sociocracy, claimed Ward, would end such weakness by bringing about the administration of government by society in its own interest. In a sociocracy "society would inquire in a business way without fear, favor, or bias [obstacles he had encountered himself in government work] into everything that concerned its welfare and if it found obstacles it would remove them, and if it found opportunities it would improve them. In a word, society would do under the same circumstances just what an intelligent individual would do. It would further in all possible ways its own interests."[25] In particular, those underprivileged people of the past who had been held back from a productive life because of limited economic and educational backgrounds would be liberated to achieve; and, in so doing, they would find personal happiness and add to the total effectiveness of society.

In a survey of the growth of government activity, Ward noted the successes of broad schemes of regulation and administration in Great Britain, Germany, and Belgium. At home, he offered the examples of the post office and public schools as evidence of efficient public administration. The success of state roads in Europe, along with high protective tariffs and government ownership of telegraph and telephone, were also cited to prove the validity of an expanded government role. Ward's criticism of an unregulated economy rested on the observation taught him by the economist Simon Patten that the unresolved concomitant of a system of unlimited production was an unequal distribution of goods that was accompanied by unequal consumption and by ruinous fluctuations in the business cycle. The inability to consume was not the result of satiated desires but of an inefficient—and inequitable—distribution system that brought human misery and market collapse in its wake.[26]

In a sociocracy, Ward was confident, social engineering would ensure not only that every family would be assured of a minimum standard of living but that the poverty and the social conflicts it created would be eliminated. While the view was still a minority one in the late nineteenth century, Ward no more than shared the position of other leaders in the American Economic Association—men like Richard Ely and John Bates Clark—who viewed the state as a positive agency for the development of public welfare. Ward, Ely, and Bates agreed upon the need for government to set wages, prices, and production levels and to promote generally economic prosperity for the nation. Economic planning by trained experts created efficiency and public service, but Ward attempted to hedge on the possible charge of elitism by maintaining that the bureaucracy would be staffed by people from all socioeconomic backgrounds and would be politically responsible to a society with universal suffrage.

Given Ward's largely abstract description of a sociocracy, and given the fluidity of various reform efforts under the generic label of Socialism, including the more limited Socialist movement (manifested in both the Socialist Labor party and the Socialist party), it was little wonder that Ward's contemporaries, and even historians years later, were as unsure about whether or not Ward was a Socialist as they were about whether or not his sociocracy was only a genteel euphemism for Socialism. Critics from the political right were hostile to his advocacy of state planning and other types of governmental intervention in the economy; and orthodox Socialists, like spurned suitors, were bitter about his persistent rejection of Marxism and about his exasperating habit of accepting many of the goals of Socialism but scoffing at their methods and claims to scientific social analysis.

As reform activity became increasingly respectable between 1900 and 1912, Ward was bombarded with personal letters from reformers of various persuasions including many Socialists; he was asked to give talks at a number of Socialist schools and meetings; and his books were reviewed favorably in *The Worker* and *The Socialist Woman*. Moreover, excerpts from his writings were used by such professional Socialist spokesmen and organizers as Eugene Debs, Daniel DeLeon, Scott Nearing, and Ward's closest friend among the Socialists, George R. Kirkpatrick, whom he had known in earlier days as a temperance lecturer![27] In most instances, the Socialists wanted either endorsements by Ward or his favors in the form of guest lectures or sociology outlines.

The most disappointed of Ward's Socialist suitors was Henry T. Jones, a left-wing Socialist from Milwaukee who had been impressed with *Dynamic Sociology* and who had tried for over a year to convince Ward that he should join the Socialist camp as a house intellectual; in fact, Jones offered Ward three hundred dollars a month and all the profit that would be grossed from a book by him about Socialism! Ward rejected Jones, for he refused to alter his views for any man or party, rejected the idea of class polarization and revolution, and rebelled esthetically against the vituperative rhetoric of Jones's colleagues. Jones concluded that Ward was deficient in his economics and was "a bourgeois phylosopher [sic] for the capitalists."[28]

With the less dogmatic Socialists who were seeking to educate themselves, Ward was more friendly. To a Philip Minassian in Philadelphia, who gave sociology lectures from Ward's books to workers in his plant, Ward sent his photograph which was to be placed, Minassian said, above his bed with those of Karl Marx and Charles Darwin. "Philadelphia Socialists," wrote Minassian, "think of Lester F. Ward as much as they do for their Karl Marx and read his books more."[29] When Ward could work it into his schedule and when the opportunity seemed to offer him the chance to preach his own message of sociocracy, Ward accepted invitations to speak to worker gatherings in order that they might "see that their hope is in true education."[30] On that basis Ward delivered lectures to the Rand School of Social Science, the Sunrise Club in New York, and other labor forums. At the Sunrise Club, he was introduced by a "labor man" as "the wisest man perhaps that America has produced— a radical man who has not yet been arrested, and yet has not kept silent."[31]

To fit their own ideological needs, more recent interpreters of Ward have tended, inaccurately, to view Ward as a Socialist, or even as an Anarchist. Thus an independent Marxist in the 1940's contended that "Ward's conception of the sociocratic society may be included within the same interpretative framework as the 'stateless-communism' of Marxism," while a harsh critic of the influence of Marxism on scientific thought found Ward "in complete harmony with the Marxian line" and "a fellow traveler."[32] The problem in interpretation stems largely from twentieth-century ideological battles that have led protagonists and critics alike to asume that only Socialists have supported collectivist social reform and state planning in America. On the contrary, there have been a number of independent, non-Marxian proposals; and among these was Ward's sociocracy, which he viewed as a democratic and scientific alternative to the deficiencies of both the laissez-faire school and the Socialists.

While Ward was warmly sympathetic to the problems of the working class and to the goals of the Socialists, he was quite suspicious of the Marxian social analyses which violated several of his basic assumptions. As programs for political action, he wrote, "they are not scientific theories or principles and [consequently] do not belong to social science."[33] Significantly, in all of Ward's voluminous writings, there is only one passing reference to Marx;[34] and in his personal "Index Rerum," a collection of thousands of quotations Ward culled from his reading for possible later use, there is not a single citation to Marx. It was not that he had never read Marx, but he believed that American society did not fit the Marxian analysis and that efforts to employ Socialist prescriptions would frighten Americans back to a laissez-faire philosophy.

Ward believed that political party agitation was fruitless and that class revolution was even more futile. Equalization of education among members of the various social and economic classes, combined with rewards conferred in strict proportion to merit (intelligence and industry), was the only sure foundation, he believed, for a just society. Equality of opportunity as the means for determining merit, he affirmed, was more progressive for society than the artificial equality imposed by Socialism; a sociocracy recognized natural inequalities and only sought to eliminate the artificial ones. Any coup at the top of the political pyramid would be ineffective, Ward warned, if the mass base of popular opinion and understanding was not yet prepared; if it were properly developed, no political coup was necessary. "It is high time for socialists to perceive that, as a rule, they are working at the roof instead of at the foundation of the structure which they desire to erect.... Their time would be better spent in working out the basal principles which will render social reform more possible."[35] Furthermore, he argued, even social telesis could not evolve the political changes necessary for a sociocracy within a single generation. Collective economic organization was probably inevitable as society evolved, but to press for such action before opinion and institutions were prepared was "criminal."[36]

Social institutions and attitudes, Ward was convinced, responded more effectively to indirect methods like education than to direct physical confrontation to secure political or economic power. The lower classes, he reported, were so unintelligent and unorganized that they could formulate neither rational demands nor strategy:

It is painful to see them constantly resorting to violence and injustice, which alienate thousands who are naturally friendly to them. ... The working people should realize that the government is their own and will be just what they make it.... They should cease to fear and distrust it, and should seek to mold and shape it.... They need no revolutionary schemes of socialism, communism, or anarchy. The present machinery of government, especially in this country, is all they could wish. They have only to take possession of it and operate it in their own interest.[37]

Only when laborers became as intelligent as capitalists, through equal access to the world's knowledge, contended Ward, would the various socioeconomic problems of society be solved. In the meanwhile, Socialists and Spencerians, with their inadequate social analysis, were better phenomena for social scientists to study than to join.

IV *Specific Political Issues*

Ward went to greater lengths in spelling out general principles of government as an applied science than he did with specific political issues of the late nineteenth and early twentieth centuries. His reluctance to engage in partisan debates from the 1870's on stemmed from his vulnerable position within the federal bureaucracy and from his earlier experience in direct political activity. Ward never enjoyed civil service protection in employment; and, while he was generally outspoken about philosophical matters, he trimmed his partisan sails to protect himself and later the Geological Survey from periodic budgetary attacks made in retribution by the House of Representatives. On numerous occasions, Ward was forced to seek protection from friendly Republican legislators to save his job; at other times, particularly during the politically turbulent 1890's, national economic conditions and the tarnished reputation of the Geological Survey brought such major slashes in the bureau's budget that no employee sought to bring unfavorable public attention upon himself.[38]

Apart from that type of bureaucratic caution, which he practiced if not preached, Ward had shifted his basic strategy in the early 1870's. He had certainly engaged in partisan activity throughout the 1860's, for he had joined radical Republican clubs, written letters to newspapers and political journals, and harangued his fellow government clerks. Ward was in the galleries cheering for President Andrew Johnson's impeachment, speaking out for freedmen's suffrage, and advocating internal bureaucratic reforms. The heady period of the late 1860's, however, gave way to a period of reaction by the early and mid-1870's, an era marked by the corruption of the Grant administration and by the erosion at every level of the ideals of Reconstruction.

Also, during the same period, Ward had personally suffered defeat with the collapse of *The Iconoclast* and the national liberal reform movement. Combined with his new interest in science, Ward concluded that partisan activity and contemporary issues in politics were generally peripheral to the real causes of social change; for party politics was an adult form of "the puerile gaming spirit."[39] Progressive change was stoked not by the party press, reform caucuses, or even votes in Congress; it was powered by more fundamental changes in the general ideas and attitudes held by the masses. That type of change required education, rational persuasion, and practical demonstration.

On only a few of the major political issues after the 1870's did Ward make his position known; yet there is some interest in comparing these positions on temperance, railroad legislation, tariffs, Coxey's army, and the Populists with his broader theoretical opinions. While the issue of temperance in a post-prohibition and cosmopolitan era takes on the aura of moral frivolity, it was an issue of real importance in late-nineteenth-century politics. Although electoral Republicans and Democrats both tried to straddle the issue, Ward maintained a forthright position. In direct debate and in written asides, he insisted that government needed to control and to limit severely the availability of alcohol. The need for public protection, the potential loss of intellectual development, and the demonstrated loss of individual rationality were used by Ward as both a scientist and a moralist. It was not until the 1890's, by every indication, that Ward had sufficiently relaxed his moral rectitude to the point of occasionally purchasing a bottle of wine for family dinners. At that point, going all the way, he would even smoke a cigar.

On the railroad question, which repeatedly stirred American politics throughout the half century following the Civil War, Ward showed considerable interest. A portion of his work in the Bureau of Statistics was spent compiling comparative railroad data for the Atlantic nations. The evidence he found led him to advocate not only regulation of railroad rates and safety precautions, but outright government nationalization of the rails.[40] In the United States, Ward charged, railroad competition brought chaos and waste. The public would wait until railroad rates and services became unendurable, and then it would seek government assistance. While nationalization was the obvious answer in this case, Ward cautioned, it did not follow that the government should assume ownership of all enterprises that dealt with the general public. The nationalization of other public utilities might be in order, but each case should be decided on its own merits.

On the political question of the merits of a strong tariff policy, debated intensely during the Benjamin Harrison and Grover Cleveland campaigns of the late 1880's, Ward firmly supported the protariff position of Republican Harrison; and he did so not out of partisan loyalty, he contended, but because of the merits of the issue.[41] The tariff, he argued, was a legitimate function of national government, which used this indirect means to support the most advanced sector of the American economy—industry—and it thereby created employment, lifted the material level of happiness for consumers, and advanced the state of American civilization. Moreover, Ward noted, the administration of tariffs produced the experience and confidence that encouraged the government to experiment with other positive, though indirect, methods of attractive legislation. The opponents of tariffs, led by the philosophical minions of Herbert Spencer, resorted to laissez-faire arguments that led to a do-nothing government and, not incidentally, drained American wealth into British countinghouses.

One of the results of the depression of 1893 was an effort to interest Congress in the idea of public works programs to alleviate the suffering caused by unemployment. The most imaginative move in that campaign was "the petition with boots on" organized by Jacob Coxey in the spring of 1894. In an effort to dramatize both human need and the utility of a federal road-building program, Coxey unleashed his ragtag "army" of unemployed men to march from Ohio to Washington. When the decidedly moderate group finally arrived in Washington, government officials and Ward's bourgeois neighbors panicked. While the Coxey affair was still in the air, and before the demonstrators were repelled by the police for walking on the grass, Ward granted an interview with a Washington newspaper that showed his good sense.[42]

Ward urged the public to be calm since "Coxey's Army" showed no indication of disturbing public order and since its members had every right to petition Congress. Contrary to the ideas of Washingtonians, Ward suggested that "great sympathy" should be given to those men who were willing to work but who were not able to find jobs. The public, he said, should be careful to distinguish between tramps who attempted to gain a living without working and men who were compelled by stress of economic circumstance to tramp in search of both work and a living.

Ward's sympathy for dissident reform groups that urged increased responsibilities and new roles for the federal government revealed itself again with the challenge of the Populist movement to orthodox political parties and ideas. While Ward never became an enthusiastic spokesman for the new movement, as did his brothers and some of his academic friends, he scoffed at the fears of colleagues and indicated the strengths of the movement.[43] The People's party, wrote Ward, faced the new conditions of industrial society and proposed to use government in a positive fashion to solve socioeconomic problems. While the party had insufficient intelligence and experience, he observed, it was the seed of sociocratic reform. In response to an 1896 appeal to Ward from Cornell University's president, Andrew White, to work against the election of William Jennings Bryan, Ward responded that, while he had always supported the Republican party, he did not fear the Populists as White did. "They do not any of them seem to know what they are about, but the whole storm is the crude, chaotic product of these half unconscious agencies at work in the land.... I shall not draw the rash conclusion that it is all a temporary craze. I shall regard it as but the foam from a deep current that has not ceased to flow and will not cease until it is strong enough to carry the world with it, albeit this cannot happen until it assumes a form that will command the respect of statesmen."[44]

So, while Ward sympathized with the historical direction the Populists were taking, indicating his own fear of the "money power," his sense of scientific politics and his deference to an image of respectability caused him to view the Populists as social science data rather than as a cause to champion. The pace of political development moved more slowly than he wished, but he was able, he said, to draw "solace from the realization of the enormous period that it has required to develop even a troglodyte or a populist."[45]

V *An Evaluation of Ward's Political Ideas*

Despite the relative success of his own life, from poor boy on the prairie to national and even international recognition, Lester Ward was able to remember the pain his success had cost and never deified the rugged individualism of his method. He did not sentimentalize hardship, and his political theory reflected that rejection. Rather, the success myth that he preached was one for the future in which the government would supply the environmental advantages that had cost him so dearly.

Ward attacked prevailing laissez-faire theories and urged in their place an organized offensive against profound social ills by an enlightened society that used its government as its instrument for social progress. When he took the suggestive concept of a welfare state found in isolated places in American political thought, he made the unsystematized early expressions into an organized conception of a sociocracy. His assurance that man could control his own destiny won broad social acceptance in the twentieth century, for his view of such a possibility was reinforced by notable human achievements in scientific ideas and economic technology. Ward's theory neatly fit the idealistic and activist temper of the American mind.

While Ward was always interested in economic reforms and visualized himself as a spokesman for the interests of the working class, his rejection of economic determinism served to separate his theories from Marxian Socialism as well as from Spencer's and Sumner's Evolutionary Determinism. The environment was powerful, but human ideas could change it; and, by so doing, they became more powerful: "Ideas do really make, lead, and move the world, and . . . if mankind can only be put into the right mental attitude, economic conditions and all else can be safely left to take care of themselves."[46]

Not unlike mid-twentieth-century American liberals, Ward
rejected Marxian Socialism in favor of an eclectic home-grown
collectivism. He advocated neither revolution, class polarization,
equal income distribution, nor government ownership of all
production. Instead, he foresaw extensive governmental economic
and social planning and administration. In a sociocracy, there
would be vastly increased government social services and the
socialization of knowledge. The most practical work that a
sociocracy would perform was the distribution of man's intellectual heritage, and this faith in education as an equalizing
force led Ward to reject the class struggle philosophy of historical materialism. Private capital and private profits would
continue in Ward's sociocracy, but the government would insure
that all citizens had an equal educational start and would
assure the fair regulation of the democratic rules of society.
To Ward, the general social welfare took precedence over unrestrained economic and social individualism.

Ward's political theory is subject to various criticisms common to those made of the social compact and utilitarian schools,
as well as those of pragmatic theory. There was no solid anthropological data to validate his hypotheses, and his psychology
was generally simplistic. Ironically, even in his own lifetime,
Ward was criticized for his heavy use of biological analogies
and metaphors in attacking a generation of determinists who
built their case on an interpretation of nature that Ward sought
to discredit. Yet his very efforts made him vulnerable to the
slings of a new generation who were themselves statistical
determinists. A reject slip that was attached to an article that
Ward had submitted to the *Political Science Quarterly* pointed
out his dated style by stating that he was "a little farther over
in the biological direction than we are disposed to claim as
our field. . . ."[47] Covering self-doubts with a veil of figures, the
younger empiricists made statistics into the new idol.

A more valid criticism of Ward's political ideas, and one
seldom made, was his underestimation of the dangers of arrogance and social irresponsibility in bureaucratic elites and the
evils of managerial manipulation on the part of those with
power to mold the social environment. Ward erred in assuming
that future agents of a sociocracy—the technocrats—would em-

body egalitarian values and social concerns similar to those that motivated his own ideas and behavior. Unhappily, the application of science to government and to the structuring of man's environment has brought real social calamities, as well as a continuing danger, for the twentieth century. But the problem has been less in the concept of environmental engineering than in the absence of the strong sense of democratic and humanitarian values that Ward brought to the idea of positive government action.

CHAPTER 5

Sociology

I A Science Of Society

IN the spring of 1876, following his return from his Utah
expedition with Powell and his winter's reading of Francis
Bacon, Charles Lyell, Ernst Haeckel, Herbert Spencer, and
August Comte's six volume *Positive Philosophy*, Lester Ward
sat down to rewrite on a "scientific foundation" his long-standing
manuscript about social reform through education. "I had begun
to see that what I was writing was *sociology*," said Ward, "and
that I should try to do something original in that science." The
sociology of Comte was not what Ward had in mind, and
Spencer's sociology was even less in harmony with his ideas:
"I was an apostle of human progress, and I believed that this
could be greatly accelerated by society itself. I therefore wanted
a progressive sociology, and it seemed to me that that was the
science naturally adopted to its furtherance."[1]

The eventual publication of *Dynamic Sociology* in 1883 became the first American work with "sociology" in its title; and
Ward, willy-nilly, had become a "founding father" of the new-
born discipline in North America. The new subject was by
no means established—there was no delineation of what it
studied, there was no particular method upon which it operated,
and there was no body of established literature upon which
it could build. A broad concept of social science had existed
in the country since before the Civil War, largely as an early
product of Comte's revolutionary world view applied to society.
This support had led to the organization of an American Social
Science Association in 1865, but the multitude of competing
interests and personalities within the organization soon splintered
it into a variety of separate pursuits; yet before its death it
had gained limited academic recognition in the social science
106

courses initiated in 1872 by William Graham Sumner at Yale University.

Ward had had no direct contact with the social science movement, but he too was reacting to the same nineteenth-century historical influences: science, the concept of progress, and sweeping manmade social change. In his case, also, Comte was the precipitating factor; for, when Ward discovered the term "sociology" in Comte's *Positive Philosophy*, he reported that immediately "I fell in love with it."[2] To guard against any charge of emotional subjectivity, Ward was careful to build his *Dynamic Sociology* upon an impressive synthesis of all the scientific knowledge of his era. With daring intellectual bravado, Ward compressed all the natural sciences into his first volume, thus forcing his readers to scan nearly five hundred pages before they reached the point in natural evolution when something akin to society emerged. It is true, as most later commentators have maintained, that nearly all of Ward's basic ideas can be found in *Dynamic Sociology*.[3]

In later books, Ward was better able to restrain his temptation to preface every sociological idea by tracing its origins to the starry cosmos. *The Psychic Factors of Civilization* (1893), his second major sociological work, omitted most of the cosmological background in an unsuccessful effort to attract a public reading of his ideas that his earlier two volume work had never found. In *The Psychic Factors*, Ward devoted principal attention to the psychological basis for sociology in an effort to distinguish his position from that of the biologically based sociologists with whom he was often confused because of his concern with classification and his penchant for Greek neologisms. *Outlines of Sociology* (1898), his third book, was a collection of his early articles for the *American Journal of Sociology* based on his 1895 and 1896 lectures to the Hartford School of Sociology.

Pure Sociology (1903) was Ward's most finished sociological work, but it perhaps lacked the intellectual excitement of *Dynamic Sociology*. Nonetheless, *Pure Sociology* contains his most systematic coverage of society and breaks new ground by adapting much of Ludwig Gumplowicz and Gustav Ratzenhofer's "social conflict" theories to his use. *Applied Sociology* (1906) completed his major sociological publications by stressing the beneficial social applications that might be made of his "pure sociology" theory. *Applied Sociology* returned to the second volume of *Dynamic Sociology* for its thesis, but Ward incorporated new scientific evidence that had appeared in the twenty-three year interval between the two works.

The subject matter of sociology, Ward announced to his readers, was human achievement: "It is not what men are but what they do. It is not the structure but the function."[4] His emphasis was not on institutions, although he treated them as a product of achievement, but on the laws that governed the behavioral relationships of men in society. Science in the late nineteenth century was a study of evolution; to study society scientifically, therefore, Ward believed, required a similar evolutionary approach. Given that approach, he devoted particular attention to the origins and the evolution of society and to the processes that had brought them about. His method was not to conduct empirical studies himself but, by broad reading and introspection, to synthesize what passed for the best thought of his time into a coherent and systematic whole. While not opposed to the use of statistical studies, his experience in the Bureau of Statistics caused him to caution sociologists in their use of statistics; for he asserted that they tended to become pedantic and to give the appearance of mathematical precision without its reality. "Science," Ward warned, "consists in the discovery of truth and not in the accumulation of facts. . . ."[5]

According to Ward, all sociology could be divided into the two categories of pure and applied. Pure sociology was an objective theoretical study of the principles of the science, including both social statistics and social dynamics. Pure sociology was society "as it is." Applied sociology, on the other hand, demonstrated the practical application of the theoretical principles to social betterment and human happiness. Applied sociology showed man how to use artificial means to accelerate the spontaneous processes of nature for subjectively selected ends. On the basis of this dichotomy, neither Spencer nor Comte ever moved beyond pure sociology.

Human society, its social relationships and its structural institutions, Ward maintained, evolved through "genetic" and "telic" means. "Genesis" dealt with the origin and spontaneous—

or "natural"—development of structures and functions. "Telesis" referred to the conscious—or "artificial"—improvement of society by man. The genetic development of society followed a "sympodial" evolutionary model, Ward claimed, not the pattern of unilinear evolution as taught by Spencer, Sumner, and Lewis Henry Morgan. Instead of following a straight path of evolutionary change, society pursued side branches, or "sympodes," with each side branch becoming a new trunk line of development to be displaced later by other sympodes. With his sympodial concept, Ward was able to avoid some of the grosser problems caused by adherence to a unilinear theory of evolution.

Ward assumed that the spontaneous or natural development of society followed inherent laws of force running through nature. The universe, he believed, was energy; and it was constantly compounding and recompounding its various manifestations. Most basic of these laws of energy were centripetal and centrifugal force, acting much like Hegel's dialectic in producing a creative synthesis of matter and the derivative functions of matter. This "synergy," said Ward, was the universal working together of the antithetical forces of nature that produced living organisms and that governed their interaction until the development of the human mind made possible an external direction of nature's forces.

The human mind as a natural product of synergy in human evolution had a biological basis in the brain; the mind represented the complex relationships between the various forms of awareness made possible by the central nervous system. John Locke's sense perception philosophy provided Ward at this point with his basic psychological concepts. The two principal functions of the mind, he contended, were feeling and intellect. Feeling had an earlier origin than intellect, and it evolved as the mechanism by which an organism found pleasure in those functions and acts that sustained its life and pain in those that reduced its life. Feeling was dynamic; it was the energy which compelled the individual to action. Desire was the product of feeling, likewise a dynamic force of the mind, which, on the basis of memory of past sensations, attempted to regain moments of pleasure and to avoid those of pain.

Intellect, Ward claimed, was a higher and later product of

the evolution of the brain's processes; and it served as a directive agent of feeling in order to maximize pleasure and to minimize pain. Since intellect could, if properly developed and disciplined, eliminate any energy that might otherwise be wasted by the unregulated feelings, the wasteful economy of nature could be replaced by an efficient economy of mind. It was the intellect and the cumulative social heritage of intellect in the form of learning that made applied sociology possible for man through the harnessing of nature's social forces. Following self-consciousness and the slow process of gaining a reliable, scientific body of knowledge concerning nature and society, humanity was able to devise means based on the inherent forces of nature to achieve whatever ends it established for itself.

In the scientific study of society, man's social achievement, Ward distinguished between social statics and social dynamics. Social statics, which Ward borrowed from Comte, dealt with man's creation of social equilibrium through the establishment of a social order. The development of a social order was "a struggle for structure," for a way to devise social techniques for the minimal solution of human problems. Social synergy was the natural force that created all structures through the cooperation of otherwise antithetical processes of nature—like collision, conflict, competition, interaction, and eventually cooperation and organization. This process of natural forces established the pattern for the coming together of diverse ethnic and social groups. The end result was the evolution of a differentiated, but homogeneous, society; and the United States, it seems likely, was Ward's model for this theoretical history of man.

Social dynamics, the other element of Ward's dichotomy, dealt with social progress or the changes in the structure of society that enabled it to improve progressively beyond the minimal organization necessary for survival. All applied sociology was dynamic and telic in function, but social dynamics also occurred, especially in man's long past, through genetic or natural processes. The three major principles of dynamic natural processes were difference of potential, innovation, and conation. The difference of potential principle operated through the crossings of cultures whereby social assimilation and biological amalgamation occurred. Innovation referred to man's psychic power to adapt his physical and his social environment in order to bring out his latent capabilities. Conation, the third of the dynamic natural processes, was the application of effort to satisfy human desires, preserve life, and modify the environment. The result from all three principles was human achievement.

The concept of conation brought Ward to one of his chief sociological principles, however vague it may seem in retrospect— the idea of social forces. Just as all nature was powered by natural forces of organized energy, so, Ward reasoned, was society; and, just as natural science studied and sought to utilize the natural forces, so social science should study and apply the social forces. Underlying this formulation, clearly, lay Ward's assumption regarding the basic unity of humanity with nature. Ward periodically altered the terminology he used in classifying his conception of the basic social forces, but he consistently found three major types. These basic social compulsions were the ontogenetic, or preservative, forces that centered around hunger and property; the phylogenetic, or reproductive, forces that focused on the sexual drive; and the sociogenetic, or spiritual, forces that concerned more recently evolved natural desires like intellectual curiosity, esthetic sensitivity, and ethical concern.

In discussing the operations that underlay social process, Ward contended that the basic natural energy, activated through the social forces, required control before achievement could occur. Ward posited two possible methods of control: the unconscious and age-long command of nature manifested in genetic, or natural, evolution and the conscious direction by human mind engaged in telesis, or telic evolution. Nature, following its unconscious path of natural selection, was minimally effective; but it was extremely slow and very wasteful. By contrast, the conscious method of control by mind was manifestly superior since it economized time and effort through foresight and the adjustment of the means to specified ends. Individual telesis had been the most common form of telic action in the past as individuals sought to maximize their private well-being; because of the increased integration of society, however, and man's increasing social consciousness, collective telesis would gradually become dominant. The intellect of mind, as it were, created the social controls and institutions through which human feelings, on a group level, could be satisfied.

Collective telesis—the social control of the dynamic forces of nature and society through a purposeful adjustment of means to ends—constituted Ward's chief contribution to sociological thought. Ward believed, as has been pointed out, that, in the process of telic control of the social forces, the state was the most effective institution by which the conscious administration of the social process could be conducted. Yet society could not perfect its control, Ward held, until an adequate store of accurate knowledge regarding the laws of nature and society was developed—the task of the sciences—and until institutions to diffuse thoroughly that knowledge throughout society—the task of education—were effective. Once society became conscious of its desired ends and became sufficiently knowledgeable to employ collective telesis means, it would become a "sociocracy" —Ward's conception of the ideal society.

In addition to his analysis of the operations of the social forces in the origins and evolution of society, Ward was occupied with a second major sociological objective: an accurate assessment of the relationship of sociology to the other sciences. Ward was committed to the conviction that the social sciences should not become estranged from the natural sciences since all knowledge was unitary in character. The classification task was viewed by Ward as extremely critical, and, in a fashion, it established a second of his principal sociological methods—that of classification of phenomena based on their inner complexity and on their relationship to other phenomena.

Ward believed, as had Comte, that all nature was serial and filiated in its composition. In point of time and in fact of organization, natural phenomena proceeded through evolution from the homogeneous to the heterogeneous and from the simple to the complex. Each new stage of evolutionary organization rested upon the properties and laws of the stage that underlay it, even though each new level was a synthesis greater than the sum of its preceding elements. In basic units forming a progressive sequence, nature followed the order of astronomy, physics, chemistry, biology, psychology, and sociology. Each basic division, Ward held, was subdivided into more specialized fields.

To understand adequately any division of nature, a student needed to understand the basic laws of those fields that underlay his own subject of specialization; the greater his knowledge of the underlying sciences, the greater his success in understanding and controlling the natural forces of his own specific subject.

Sociology, viewed from man's inevitable anthropomorphic stance, was the highest and most complex science. Man was the highest and most complex unit of nature, and his present social organization was the most complex in his evolutionary development. To study sociology required an intimate knowledge of the mind, man's most highly evolved physical structure; for the mind provided much of the basic content of sociological subject matter through the human desires that constituted the social forces. Biology, too, though subordinate to psychology, was an essential background science to the study of society; but biological evolution, Ward repeatedly insisted, was not analogous to contemporary social evolution. To be a sociologist was no simple matter, and it required students of broad scientific background. Students, Ward believed, should not study sociology until graduate school and then only people with keen ability to generalize and to grasp the complex relationships in nature might successfully make this subject their specialization. The simple truths of sociology, however, in diluted and applied fashion could, he held, probably be taught at lower educational levels. The necessary background and mental talents for a sociologist, not coincidentally, were those that Ward saw in himself.

Aware of the fragmentation of the social science field, with its scramble for territorial claims, conceptual principles, and title to hierarchial authority, Ward boldly asserted that sociology was the supreme generalizing social science. Anthropology, political science, ethics, and economics were subordinate social sciences that furnished the data that the more comprehensive sociology coordinated and used as the basis of its generalizations. Consequently, Ward's sociology class, "A Survey of All Knowledge," at Brown University made pedagogical sense from his perspective of the filiation of the sciences.

Within this broad field of generalization devised by Ward, two areas merit a more extended treatment: Ward's critique of a conservative application of Darwinian evolutionary theory to society and his elaboration of the artificial stratification of society.

II   Social Darwinism

Two books that embodied quite divergent social interpretations of evolutionary theory appeared in 1883: Lester Ward's *Dynamic Sociology* and William Graham Sumner's *What Social Classes Owe to Each Other*.[6] These two works established for nearly a generation the perimeters within which sociologists and other social commentators argued the applicability of evolution in the natural sciences to the human field of society. Scores of rival interpretations emerged in the scholarly and, more often, not so scholarly controversy that was later incorporated by historians under the general rubric of "social Darwinism."[7]

One of the best known of these interpretations, the conservative, laissez-faire formulation championed by Herbert Spencer, had its most articulate American spokesman in Sumner. The Yale professor was the same age as Ward, but he had spent the Civil War years as a ministerial student at Gottingen and had shortly thereafter accepted his prestigious Ivy League professorship. Ward had little in common by way of temperament, academic success, or ideological commitment with the aristocratic Sumner who equally mistrusted the activity of government and of social reformers. Like Spencer, Sumner believed that the operation of the natural laws of evolution were omnipotent—and that man intervened only to his own detriment. While not personally an apologist for the harsher features of the competitive economic system in America, Sumner's brand of social science, which emphasized the power and morality of social custom, as well as that of natural law, led to an acceptance of things as they were.

Ward could not resist doing battle with this "final wail against the modern practices of states and peoples" that was the epitome of the laissez-faire doctrine that he had attacked in *Dynamic Sociology*. In a review of Sumner's work, Ward found a fallacy in every proposition of his sociological antagonist.[8] At the heart of Ward's critique of Sumner's conservative social Darwinism from the perspective of his meliorist social Darwinism were three major criticisms. First, charged Ward, since Sumner was not a biologist, he did not realize that ability to survive in Darwin's world of natural selection was wholly distinct from real superiority; for the crude power of thistles, rats, and stinging insects enabled them to overpower other life with whom they competed for environmental sustenance. Second, Sumner failed to realize that the natural evolution of man's mind gave him the transcendent power to break the stranglehold of wasteful genetic evolution and to accelerate the natural forces in directions that fulfilled man's unique purposes. Third, claimed Ward, history and daily experience demonstrated that man was already following this truth and that with increased social organization—demonstrated by the success of public schools, post offices, and transportation—society would become even more successful in utilizing artificial selection to advance its civilization.

To do nothing but mind one's own business, as Sumner advised, would be "nihilistic and suicidal," charged Ward. The social results of Sumner's biologically based sociology, contending as he did that the laws of biology were incumbent upon man, were especially severe on the poor and on the working class, Ward noted. Since Sumner assumed that the favors of the world were by natural law distributed according to merit, he logically concluded that the poor received all they deserved and were incapable of a better life. For Ward, of course, this concept was a direct attack not only on his own ideas but on his very existence.

Ward's preferred antagonist in debating the social meaning that should be deduced from the processes of natural evolution was not Sumner but Herbert Spencer. In many respects, Ward built his career on an extended criticism of the political and ethical conclusions of the English philosopher. For over a quarter of a century and through every publication in which he could gain entry and through every argument that he could muster, Ward attacked the "gospel of inaction" and the social pessimism that he believed Spencer's laissez-faire philosophy produced. Much of that debate has already been examined in discussing Ward's ideas on education and government where his views differed most sharply with Spencer's. But in science, Ward could never fathom why Spencer failed to apprehend that the evolutionary processes were split in twain with the evolution of the brain which, Ward reiterated, made possible a new type of humanly directed evolution.

When natural processes were given free reign, Ward warned in attempting to turn Spencer's argument on itself, the result was only temporary free competition. Quite quickly in animal and plant life, he argued, competition was succeeded by the superior powers driving all else out and gaining a complete monopoly over a sector of the environment. If society were left to those same natural laws, human monopolies of economic power would arise to destroy the very individualism that Spencer sought to protect. Spencer was logically inconsistent, Ward claimed, in not applying his principle of evolutionary integration into the social sphere as he did all other natural processes. For, paradoxically, without social integration through government, with the regulation and planning that the state could provide society, human liberty and the individualism it fostered would fall victim to the monopolistic products of unrestrained natural evolution.[9]

It is apparent in Ward's continuing debate with Spencer and other proponents of the superiority—or inevitability—of the biological modes of evolutionary process that his monistic assumptions led him to accept along with his opponents the belief that there was a direct application of natural law processes to human society. These processes had existed in the past and would continue into the future, Ward believed, unless man utilized the intelligence his own particular evolution provided to break the control of humanly purposeless natural forces.

Ward was less easily able, however, to argue his way past the treacherous monistic temptation to view society as analogous to a biological organism. Arguing by analogy was a common and logically slippery practice among sociologists of the period, and the social organism was a favorite analogy that could be used in many ways. Spencer, in particular, had used it to compare social institutions with various functions of a biological organism in order to point out the apparent natural basis of society. To protect himself from the trap of discovering that an organism's brain could be used by analogy to justify the centralizing directive functions of government, Spencer confessed that his analogy broke down when it came to the central nervous system. In an organism, he admitted, there was only a single consciousness; individual cells were not sentient and were incapable of feeling. In society, however, there was no single consciousness and only the individual members were capable of feeling. In an organism, the cells existed for the benefit of the collective entity because only it could feel, while in a society the reverse was the case. Consequently, Spencer held, government could not be used as the natural analogue of the brain.

Ward, in most instances, was wary of the organismic analogy because of its use by conservatives to remind lesser peoples to follow dutifully their ordained function in the life of society; and, as a professional biologist, Ward was also fully aware of the inapplicable features of the analogy. But Spencer's problem in logic about the central nervous system was too great a temptation, and Ward accepted the pragmatic aid of the organismic analogy to highlight the processes of society in favor of his position. The brain, he instructed Spencer, did so provide a natural analogue with centralized government; and, since government in all societies was much less organized than the brain of any organism, there was evident need for greater social evolution. He agreed with Spencer's exceptions to the analogy, but he countered their use in depreciating the role of government by arguing that in society it was only through complete social integration that liberty and fullest consciousness were possible for the individual; therefore, Spencer's very exception gave the support of nature to the utility of government.[10]

In confronting a pragmatic and intellectually impatient society, Ward's more successful and less subtle line of attack on Spencer's social evolutionism continued to be a demonstration of the disastrous consequences should man—and now society—refrain from interfering with nature. The amenities of civilization, he rightfully insisted, were all artificial alternations of Spencer's nature:

When a well-clothed philosopher on a bitter winter's night sat in
a warm room well lighted for his purpose and writes on paper with
pen and ink in the arbitrary characters of a highly developed
language the statement that civilization is the result of natural laws,
and that man's duty is to let nature alone so that untrammeled it
may work out a higher civilization, he simply ignores every circumstance of his existence and deliberately closes his eyes to every fact
within the range of his faculties. If man had acted upon his theory
there would have been no civilization, and our philosopher would
have remained a troglodyte.[11]

Throughout Ward's protracted debate with Spencer, until the
latter's death in 1903, Ward never used nor saw the phrase
"social Darwinism" applied either to Spencer or to himself.
Ward usually referred to the Spencerian school as "biological
sociologists," but he also indicated its liberation from the constraints of genetic natural processes. Much of the debate between
Ward and Spencer did hinge on the social application of
evolutionary theory, but the reliance of both men on the explanations of Lamarck might as logically have led to the general
label of "social Lamarckianism." Moreover, Ward's common
incorporation of arguments that were drawn from geological
processes and of analogies that were based on geological phenomena in his sociology could as easily have warranted the
designation of "social Lyellism" after the renowned British
geologist Charles Lyell.

It was not until 1905 that Ward discovered "social Darwinism," he records; and then he first found use of the phrase
on the continent of Europe—although it swiftly made its way
to the annual meeting of the American Sociological Society in
late 1906.[12] The social Darwinism that Ward found in Europe
was manifested in two schools of sociologists who used the
term to malign their ideological opponents. Socialist social
scientists, led by the Italian economist Achille Loria, applied
the term to Malthusian apologists for capitalism in the economic
struggles of the day; but the pacifist sociologists, led by the
Russian reformer Jacques Novicov, used the phrase invidiously
to attack the "race conflict" school of sociologists as proponents
of war.

Ward found both these uses of the phrase "social Darwinism"

unacceptable, and he strongly criticized those who so used it—
especially after he discovered that Novicov had denounced him
as a war-mongering "social Darwinist" because of his favorable
treatment of the social conflict theorists in *Pure Sociology*.[13]
Much to Ward's professed surprise, he found the phrase being
used in still a third fashion in the United States by a sociologist
at Dartmouth, Collin Wells, to describe favorably an examination of the influence of contemporary social institutions upon
the biological quality of the American population.[14] No doubt
Ward would have been even more amazed to find historians a
half century later referring to him as a "*reform* social Darwinist."

The problem with all those who used the expression, Ward
insisted, was that their descriptions of what constituted "social
Darwinism" had little or nothing to do with what Darwin taught.
Few people claimed the label to describe themselves, and any
who did knew even less of the principles of natural selection
enunciated by Darwin. Instead, the phrase was being used to
set up straw men that could easily be demolished and thus
promote the particular cause of those who raised the term. In
the process, Darwin was being besmirched as an advocate of
capitalist exploitation and war, while the principle of natural
selection was being caricaturized into a bloody drama of predator
and prey or into an alternate version that ignored man's recent
control of environmental forces. Ward was able to dismiss quite
quickly these interlopers on to a field of evolutionary sociology
that he and Spencer had cultivated as their proprietary domain
for several decades, but he could not as easily ignore the conflicts apparent in contemporary social stratification that had
prompted the "social Darwinian" metaphor.

III   *Social Stratification: Race and Class*

The field of social stratification in sociology emerged only
after Lester Ward's death and during his life he devoted only
minor attention to the ways in which societies established differentiated population classifications. Yet Ward's highly refined
concern about status and about the objective importance of
classification schemes based on race and class in American life
did lead him to consider the nature and causes of these phe-

nomena. Throughout his discussions of race and class, despite occasional lapses into the hierarchical terminology of the evolutionary naturalists, Ward attacked the prevailing beliefs that behavioral differences in races and in classes were hereditary, that the races had separate origins, and that racial or class amalgamation would produce biological and cultural degeneration. There was no proof, he preached, of differential intellectual capacity among the races and classes. It was even clearer, he affirmed, that "there is no race and no class of human beings who are incapable of assimilating the social achievement of mankind and of profitably employing the social heritage."[15] While Ward can legitimately be charged with rigidity in his sociological ideas, his stubborn refusal to submit to the blandishments of newer racist and classist sociological interpretations— while he was continuing to search for scientific supports for his democratic assumptions—preserved an island of hope for humanity in a sea of thundering pessimism.

The nature of race and its social significance had been a matter of profoundest concern for the young Ward. Engaged in abolition debates before the Civil War and in battlefield combat during the war over slavery, he displayed much more than an academic interest in the question of race. He later recalled that his earliest knowledge of race and the social meaning ascribed to it came from an engraving in his elementary geography book that showed a plantation owner mistreating his black slaves.[16] His subsequent Abolitionist views and his emotional sympathy for Negroes, he reported, stemmed from this early identification with the abused workers of the illustration. In academy essays, often of crude satire, Ward as a young man rejected biblical explanations for racial differences and slavery; instead, he tied such conceptions to the economic and social power of aristocracies. Slaveowners became brutish barbarians from their power, he concluded, while subordinate slaves became ignorant "niggers."[17]

Ward had his first real contact with black Americans while serving in the army in Virginia and while setting up housekeeping in Washington, D. C. On these occasions, Ward assumed the usual white power position of employer by hiring black domestics; but, at the same time, he attended the political rallies of Frederick Douglass and urged the adoption of black suffrage by his Treasury Department colleagues. Lizzie Ward attended normal school classes for a term at Howard University; and, although she later attempted to gain a teaching position in a black school, she could find none. However, she and Lester did tutor their black housekeeper, Clarissa Reader, who strongly desired to learn to read and who, Ward reported, was a very conscientious worker. The various forms of racial exploitation which shaped the lives of American black people were clearly manifest to Ward because of the experiences of his domestics. These experiences were not limited to the exclusion of education during slavery days for they happened contemporaneously in Ward's household when a grocer sold a second housekeeper stale bread for a cent more a loaf than the grocer charged white customers and when Ward's white roomer seduced that same housekeeper.[18]

On the basis of these experiences and his commitment to human opportunity, Ward penned an article on the races in 1868.[19] Racial superiority, he wrote, was not determined by color but by moral and intellectual faculties. Negroes, in that day, did not exhibit as high a rating as whites, Ward conceded; but their essential quality was proved not by present condition but by the potential of their natural endowment. Blacks under as favorable circumstances as whites would develop a civilization of as high an order as any in Europe, he claimed. Their civilization would not be precisely similar to Europe's; but, what their civilization lacked in one particular, it would make up in another. While there might be distinctions in certain faculties between the two races, there was "no reason to declare the one superior to the other...."

It was quite evident, Ward explained, that the environmental circumstances—geographical and social—had not been equal for the races. The African race had developed under an enervating tropical climate—one geographically separated from the cultural and trade patterns of the past two thousand years. Thinly scattered in population and divided into hostile factions, there had been little opportunity for the support or the peace necessary to protect learning. While the geographical conditions were improved in America, the social conditions of slavery had been so abject that it was considered a crime for the blacks to receive knowledge. "The only wonder," noted Ward, "is that they have not sunk lower into barbarism and degradation; and the very fact that they have not, argues well for their inborn talents and their natural mental and moral endowments."

While Negroes were quite uncultivated at present, Ward contended that in a few generations substantial change could occur. To support his thesis, he pointed out the differences in intellectual and cultural traits between the ancient Romans and contemporary Italians and between the German barbarians of the Classical period and present-day Germans. In each case, he argued, it was not a matter of the race's changing but of different historical circumstances. Whites, he said, had been savages longer than they had been civilized; and black Africans had furnished the world all the civilization it possessed for a longer period than they had been sunk in barbarism. To understand the essential equality of the races, therefore, he cautioned, one needed the long view of historical perspective, not the short view of present prejudices.

No doubt it was Ward's long view and the strength of his original emotional commitment to the proposition that human talent was no function of either race or class that saved him from the disillusionment and the reactionary racism that beset many prewar racial egalitarians in the late nineteenth century. Ward had not expected as rapid a transformation of freedmen as had other nineteenth-century liberals. As it was, however, Ward shifted attention after the 1860's to the seemingly more pressing problems of class exploitation. "My matured sympathies," he wrote Andrew White in 1896, "have been transferred from the negro to the proletariat in general including the negro."[20] Little attention was paid to race in *Dynamic Sociology*, but Ward—adopting the thought habits of social evolutionists like Lewis Henry Morgan—did note that the contemporary progress of the "lower races" was being checked by the power of the "higher races" who were refusing to permit such improvement. While his analysis of slavery now gave it partial credit for developing in the blacks their habits of industry and discipline, as taught by Spencer, he was careful to except "our own exotic chattel slavery that had none of the redeeming qualities of the primitive institution."[21]

The Neo-Lamarckian and Neo-Darwinian controversy late in the century refocused Ward's interest in matters of race. By stressing the continuing operation of the social environment in ameliorating any nonutilitarian biocultural characteristics of race groups, Ward viewed Neo-Lamarckianism as more socially hopeful than the hereditarian racism of those Americans who embraced Weismann's findings. While Lamarckianism, too, had been used by many to explain the origins of the presumed biological and cultural characteristics of the races, Ward chose to see Lamarck's doctrine as one that provided a basis for an egalitarian future through social effort.

Following Ludwig Gumplowicz's lead, Ward theorized in *Pure Sociology* that the natural evolution of man was character- ized by the conflict and conquest pattern of ever larger popula- tion groups coming into contact with other human groups exhibiting different cultural and racial characteristics. In these historical conquests and in modern colonial wars, the issue of battle depended little on character or intelligence but on narrow specializations such as the cultivation of the arts of war. In all other respects, the conquered race might be superior to the conquering race, argued Ward. While the conquering race often enslaved the conquered, both learned from one another; and their relationship became in time one of caste and class instead of slavery. The conquerors divided into the castes of governors, priests, and warriors; the conquered became the laborers; and a group intermediate in function and in biological amalgamation became a business and trade caste. When mutual economic needs, inevitable racial amalgamation fostered by the charm of sexual novelty, and the need for unified protection against the threat of outside enemies eventually wore down the feelings of race superiority and the organization of a caste system, the result was the emergence of a new race.[22]

Since man had emerged, Ward continued, there had been so many "collisions and conjugations" of the races that no historical people were any longer racially pure. From a biological and a cultural standpoint, this lack of purity was a good thing. The English, for example, were a race composed in historic times of at least six major assimilations. The same was true, although with less harmonious results and with a greater residue of racial prejudice, in Austria where the conflict principle had been first enunciated by Gumplowicz. Every assimilation, said Ward, was a fresh "cross-fertilization" of cultures and biological types that led to advances in social achievements and in physical capacities. The most "efficient" races, he reported, were those that had never been separated from the flow of other cultural groups. It was not a matter of mental inferiority, therefore, for the less advanced races "only lacked the opportunity which comes through the struggle of races and repeated assimilations."[23]

Gumplowicz's similar theory of social evolution through racial conflict, with much stronger racist conclusions, had been based on a polygenetic theory of human origins. From this conception of the independent origins of the various races, Ward sought to dissuade Gumplowicz during their 1903 meeting at Graz. Ward, as a biologist, lectured his Austrian colleague on the extreme biological unlikelihood of parallel skeleton, muscular, and nervous systems having evolved separately among the human races. The great variety of external forms within the physiological and psychological unity of mankind was a result, he expounded, of gradual adaptation to the various climates and modes of life required by geographic conditions. The long era of human differentiation had been reversed during historical times; and, in the present geological era, humanity was moving into a long period of integration. Thoroughly admonished and partially bewildered by a sociologist who calmly spoke of social processes in geological time frames, Gumplowicz confessed that "I was beaten. I stood there like a pupil who had just been thoroughly whipped by his teacher."[24]

The idea of biological integration became an important element in Ward's conception of the future. Drawn to sociological prediction by his work on *Applied Sociology* and by his own old age, Ward began to project in lectures before the International Institute of Sociology, in articles, and in his last book the conception of a continuing evolution in which all races would be fused and all humankind would be undifferentiated by racial markings. A single homogeneous and completely assimilated race, "the human race," he forecast, would emerge in which would be represented all the superior characteristics of its racial components. Only at that point, he announced, could a true society be achieved based on equality without distinctions, prejudices, or stratification. It would take a long time to achieve, he acknowledged to Mrs. Cape, "but not so long as it took to develop the horse."[25]

A number of educated, upwardly mobile black Americans were attracted to Ward's teachings because of his assumptions regarding racial equality and upward advancement through education and effort but also because of his social conflict theories. On several occasions during the 1890's, Ward addressed convocations of black students in the Washington area on the topic "Opportunity versus Heredity." Requesting a repeat of this lecture, one black school principal wrote, "It is peculiarly inspiring to us as members of the Colored Race for we have so little to gain from the past. Our opportunities have just begun and we want to be thoroughly prepared to meet and master them."[26] On another occasion, introduced by the first black United States senator, Blanche K. Bruce, Ward delivered the same lecture to all the black teachers in Washington, D. C., at their request. Similarly, Ward addressed graduate sociology clubs of black students at Howard University and corresponded with other black students who requested additional information. And at least one black student at Columbia University was impressed by Ward's work when it was introduced in a sociology class by Franklin Giddings; for Chandler Owen, as A. Philip Randolph later recalled, brought Lester Ward to him and he brought Karl Marx to Owen when the pair teamed up during the teens of the twentieth century to organize black political councils and economic unions.[27]

More typical of Ward's influence on race thinking, however, was the black high school principal in Texas who wrote Ward that he had read all his books. "Truly, I am unknown to you but you are by no means unknown to me.... Your argument in Applied Sociology respecting the capacity of races is my philosophic hope—as a black man, or rather a man, black.... *I* feel that *I* am indebted to you for the hopeful doctrine that you have given the world, not for my race as such, but for all struggling humanity endeavoring to rise thru meritorious effort."[28] Considered quite liberal, if not radical, for his day, Ward's views on race stratification provided educated black Americans with a feasible rallying point.

When it came to an examination of class, or the socioeconomic stratification of society, Lester Ward's views were as fully conditioned by the conflicts in American society and by his hopes for "meritorious effort" as were his ideas on race.[29] Ward acknowledged the existence of social groupings based on economic and educational power, and he never denied his sympathy with the lower classes. The working class, or the proletariat (as he later called it after increased exposure to European analyses), were certainly exploited economically and were restricted in their life chances by a denial of adequate education. But there was too much of the American romantic democrat in Ward, along with the existential fact of his own modest success, to adopt the militant stance on class advocated by Marxian sociologists and by his Socialist correspondents.

In fact, the origins of class was not treated systematically by Ward until the appearance of *Pure Sociology* at the turn of the century when—beset by his own declining economic prospects in the Geological Survey, his failure to find an academic post in either sociology or paleobotany, and his fears that the increasingly critical reviews of his writing were the work of the "money power"—he adopted with modifications the social conflict analysis of Gumplowicz and Ratzenhofer. That analysis, previously described in the discussion on race, held that social classes were the evolutionary product of race conflict and subjugation as social evolution moderated the relationships of conquered and conqueror to the point that caste and later class relationships based on differentiated rights and duties developed.[30] Because the process of conflict and accommodation, Ward believed, was a continuous one, each present-day society occupied a different position on the social evolutionary spectrum relative to the time of its origin and the rate of its social processes.

The bases for these social processes, or "social karyokinesis" in Ward's inimitable phraseology, were economic interests that sprang from the ontogenetic social forces of hunger and self-protection. A detailed examination of those forces, he believed, revealed the origins and functions of exploitation, slavery, labor, property, production, and distribution. Belief in the continuous evolution of the product of these social forces led Ward to consistently oppose the political and the economic conservatives who, he believed, sought to enshrine the contemporary social order as either divinely ordained or as a "naturally" established product of other forces outside of man's control. Since social classes and their functions were the product of man's conflicts and conquests, Ward was convinced that human actions could moderate and eventually destroy the disparate life chances and personal happiness that were generated by social class membership.

Ward was never consistent in detailing the number or nature of social classes in America, and his borrowings from the European conflict theorists were of virtually no utility in clarifying his confusion, or that of other American sociologists, regarding the nature of American social stratification. Depending on the context, Ward from *Dynamic Sociology* to *Applied Sociology* variously deduced two, three, four, five, and more classes in America. Interestingly enough, Ward found room in most of his enumerations for an intermediate class of talent upon whose achievements other classes both higher and lower depended; this "middle-class" compulsion on the part of so many late-nineteenth-century reformers was confirmed in Ward's case by his many efforts to maintain a position of respectability in Washington society that was associated with middle class life.

Despite Ward's hunger for social approbation, or perhaps because of it, he was ever ready, however, to castigate the upper classes for the privilege and power they maintained at the expense of the toiling lower classes. His description of the "principle of deception" by which ruling groups maintained power and status by fraud, disguise, and pretense was incorporated by Thorstein Veblen in *The Theory of the Leisure Class,* a work from which Ward derived great satisfaction.[31] Ward and Veblen were fully convinced that class distinctions played an important role in American life; and, because of the degree to which they then operated, they contributed to the inefficient organization of society.

Particularly grievous to Ward's sensibilities and to his theory of the dynamics of society was the extent to which education in the past had been the monopoly of the upper classes. Since Ward, unlike Marxists and other evolutionary naturalists, conceptualized society as a pyramid with *knowledge* as the base and economic technology as the *superstructure*, to deprive the masses of knowledge not only limited their ability to find happiness through the satisfaction of their basic desires but minimized as well the opportunities for social advancement of all members of society. Without knowledge, the preservation of error held all back from true understanding of nature and of the new ideas needed to facilitate man's exploitation of nature. Education was not merely one of many social side effects of one's class position; it was a basic determinant of that position.

Following the logic of his presuppositions, it was only natural for Ward to reject the idea that class position was a product of one's ability. More precisely, Ward held that talent was broadly scattered through all classes and that only birth and environmental circumstances produced pecuniary inequalities. In America, there was some chance, he believed, for people to improve their class position through the opportunity of public education and through heroic individual effort. But counteracting this possibility was the capacity of the upper class to reinforce its position by exploiting the ignorance of the masses while insuring that its own children alone received an adequate education. In more rigid class societies, censorship was imposed on the knowledge permissible to the lower classes, while in slave societies nearly all knowledge was denied subordinate peoples.

Given Ward's biases and his previously discussed ideas on education and government, it should come as no surprise to find that he, like most essentially middle class intellectual reformers, sought for the future a single class society—some reformers euphemistically called it a "classless" society—that was modelled on idealized notions of the current upper middle class. In his conception of such a unified society, Ward viewed equal access to education through public schools and to the power of the state by a technocracy of applied sociologists—reminiscent of Comte's Positivist priests—as sufficient social force to terminate the inequities of the present class society.[32] But, when moving from diagnosis to prescription, Ward, like other sociological reformers, adopted a lexicography of vagueness to cloak the uncertainty of his prediction.

In matters of class, as of race, Ward approached the subject in terms of a social problem requiring ameliorative action through increased social cohesiveness and the eventual abandonment of social distinctions based on considerations other than of merit. Despite protestations that his was a dispassionate and objective account of the social processes, Ward, like Veblen and a substantial majority of subsequent American sociologists, approached the subject with highly sensitized ethical concerns that befitted a discipline which replaced an earlier moral philosophy.[33] Consistency in matters of class analysis was not a strong point in Ward's account, due partly, to be sure, from the amorphousness of American class patterns and the limited utility of European analyses based on dissimilar historical experience. Nor was Ward able to accept the extent to which the powers and agencies of government operated in particular class interests; furthermore, he displayed overconfidence in the willingness of the powerful to relinquish their power and in the ability of universal education to dissolve class lines. Even more painful to admit about Ward's observations on class, however, was his lack of self-reflection to see that his personal pursuit of silk suits, Chickering grand pianos, and social propriety was an example of the emulation of conspicuous consumption and of honorific observances that his colleague, Thorstein Veblen, had so rightly ridiculed in the leisure class.

IV *An Evaluation*

Until American sociologists' recent rediscovery of social theory and their own history, they tended from 1920 to 1960 to view Ward as the system-builder windmill against which their empiricist lances were tilted;[34] for evolutionary social theory and introspection as a social science methodology had assuredly become unfashionable. Even Ward in his own day had left himself open to criticism by his vague terminology which occasionally seemed to border on empty verbalisms; whole arguments were mounted on the basis of reified neologisms. "Synergy," "creative synthesis," "conation," the distinction between "pure" and "applied" and that between "static" and "dynamic" all seemed to take their meaning from the context in which they were used rather than from any inherent reality. Even the very basic concept of "social forces" was never clearly specified by demonstrable processes or by qualities in society. Other concepts like "function" and "process" were used in mutually exclusive fashions within the same work, and logical classifications were confused with ontological reality. While not denying the importance of either synthetic theory or introspective generalizations, it does seem a pity that Ward consistently ignored a systematic observation of an available functioning society in favor of ingenious speculation about a hypothetical prehistoric society.

Ward increased his vulnerability by his proclivity to apply a methodology, a terminology, and mental habits acquired from his work in paleobotany—especially his classification compulsion—to the new field of sociology. In this way, he increased the confusion that often associated him with biological sociology and with an organismic theory for which he was not so responsible as some critics supposed.[35] Even more damaging to the durability of his sociological ideas was his reliance on an evolutionary anthropology and on a pleasure-pain psychology that were found misleading and inaccurate even before his death.

Seldom mentioned, however, in any critical assessment of Ward's work, often because critics shared the same ambitions, was the danger in Ward's world view of perceiving sociology as a paternalistic "administrative" social science composed of an elite group of social theorists and technicians who themselves, or through others whom they would advise, might manipulate "social control" for a social good that in reality was little more than their personal interest and prejudices. The sociology and anthropology that grew up in the Washington, D. C., area associated with the federal government, as in the Bureau of American Ethnology, was particularly prone to such self-conceptualization, although the lives and work of Edward Ross and Franklin Giddings demonstrate that the temptation was not limited to those within the shadow of Washington political power. Ward's own democratic values minimized this Comtean precedent in his theory, but the danger remained.

But, having admitted all this, there remains a great deal that was of real sociological value in Ward's work. Much of this value has been missed by later sociological critics since the ideas and assumptions initially enunciated by Ward became the unconscious starting point for subsequent American sociology. Ward's overriding contribution to social theory was his proposition that man did not have to wait for the wasteful, inhumane, and sluggish methods of natural evolution and of laissez-faire social theory; man could exercise purposeful change through knowledge and social organization. The same belief in man's potential conquest over the constraints of either nature's inertia or the impediments of human prejudice sustained Ward in his attacks on the social inequities created by American ideas about both race and class.

Ward's early sociological works and friendships helped stimulate an interest among aspiring sociologists to create a science of society, as his correspondence with Small, Ross, Giddings, Cooley, Veblen, and Dealey suggests.[36] While many of Ward's specific formulations were abandoned in the twentieth century, as astute a judge of the course of sociology in America as Albion Small remarked after Ward's death that "I have often said, and it remains my estimate, that, everything considered, I would rather have written *Dynamic Sociology* than any other book that has ever appeared in America."[37] Ward had saved a generation of American sociologists, testified Small, from following Spencer's "misconstrued evolutionism" that English sociology was still striving to overcome as an influence. Small might also have added that Ward's *Psychic Factors of Civilization* had helped direct the attention of American sociology to the psychological basis of human and social behavior, a distinguishing characteristic of sociology for many years in the United States.

Credit should also be given to Ward's valiant, if unsuccessful, effort to avoid the alienation of the social from the natural sciences in modern scholarship. The separation of the two in the twentieth century, partly caused by the real need of sociologists to establish a concept of culture divorced from biology, has produced more than its share of the compartmentalization of knowledge; confused academic and public policy; and, most especially, created mutual hostilities that have exacerbated

stereotypes about the nonhumane nature of the natural sciences
and the unreliability of the social sciences. Much the same
judgment can be made of Ward's efforts to integrate the variety
of disparate sociological concepts into a synthetic and coherent
whole. He may have failed, and failed grandly, in establishing
a general theory that could survive his death; but the twentieth-
century mania for specialization and empiricism has amply
demonstrated that, unless each generation makes the effort
to integrate knowledge and its values, personal alienation and
social discontinuity are the result.

Finally, the most important contribution of Ward to American
sociology, aside from his repudiation of the laissez-faire and the
conservative social Darwinist social philosophies, was the legitimacy he helped provide an academically and psychologically
insecure discipline. By virtue of his early sociological publications, especially *Dynamic Sociology,* and his solid position in
an established natural science, Ward furnished the first genera-
ation of American sociologists with a foundation in time and
space. Albion Small, the major entrepreneur of the discipline
from his seat of power as chairman of the first sociology department in the nation at the University of Chicago and as the
founder and editor of the *American Journal of Sociology,* displayed not only his own early conceptual indebtedness to Ward
but his Yankee shrewdness when he invited Ward to become
an advisory editor of the journal and to fill its pages during
its first decade with successive articles that testified to the
scientific character and place of sociology among the various
sciences.

Ward shared with the first generation of American sociologists
a background that included the highly sensitized ethical and
moral concerns of incipient social reformers—preachers without
orthodox religious faith—and the closely related personal tension
of men who were reared in the values and social context of
rural small town America only to find their mature lives in
strikingly dissimilar urban centers. But Sumner, Small, Ross,
Giddings, Cooley, Veblen, and countless lesser lights did not
have a background of knowledge and of reputed professional
stature in a "real" science as did Ward, and so he functioned
to supply the felt need for the movement.

In the lean early years of the 1890's, Ward's books and articles helped remedy the dearth of a professional literature for academic visibility and classroom use. A decade later, it was Ward who was encouraged by his younger colleagues to initiate their organizational break from the American Economic Association. Ward, as a lifetime member of the parent organization, had sparred with economists since the 1880's over the relationship of economics to sociology; and from the 1890's he tangled almost annually at their meetings with Simon Patten, a foremost economics spokesman. It was appropriate, therefore, when Ward at the 1905 economics meeting in Baltimore made the motion for sociologists to separate from the economists by forming their own professional organization. And it was not out of mistaken notions of Ward's contributions to the field that the first meeting of the seceding sociologists, supported particularly by Giddings, Small, Cooley, and Ross, elected Ward by acclamation to the presidency of the American Sociological Society.[38] Rather, their support was a product of "consciousness of kind" and "the looking-glass self" that came home to roost.

Sociologists recognized that Ward supplied the basic needs of the new organization by providing a symbol who personified mature intellectual dignity, a long and esteemed background in both the natural and social sciences, and the international respectability that American parvenu sociologists sought to acquire. Furthermore, Ward was a politically acceptable candidate to provide unity among a membership that was marked by exaggerated egos, conceptual quarrels, and personal rivalries that made Ward, who suffered the same disabilities, look exemplary by comparison.

Despite the growing repudiation of Ward's evolutionary concerns by the time of his death and despite the subsequent shift in sociological fashions away from social theory, Ward had played a major role in establishing basic assumptions in the American sociological movement. A paper by Albion Small in 1906 that set forth four major points of agreement among sociologists seems conceptually to outline Ward's basic position.[39] American sociologists, reported Small, accepted the task of searching for scientific laws of human behavior that resembled the natural laws governing physical phenomena. They viewed social change as social evolution, he added, interpreting it as progress toward a better society. Furthermore, they regarded social progress as amenable to acceleration by direct human intervention through a knowledge of sociological laws. And, finally, Small concluded in his summary of contemporary sociological beliefs, sociologists conceived social behavior to be the product of the dynamic nature of individual behavior. Ward's specific sociological ideas were becoming dated, but his assumptions had shaped the major focus of American sociology.

CHAPTER 6

A Gospel of Science

I *Social And Intellectual Origins*

LESTER Ward, like many other Americans, found the Gilded Age a period of deep spiritual crisis. By penning anticleric and freethought editorials in his Rhode Island Avenue residence, Ward suggested the temper of the religious times as well as did Lucy Hayes, the first lady of the land, by inviting passersby off nearby Pennsylvania Avenue to join the Hayes's for a Sunday evening of hymns in the East Room of the White House. A sociointellectual revolution, scarcely realized at the time, was at work secularizing Protestant American society. Spawned by the continuing influence of rationalist thought and a growing faith in science as the ultimate criterion for truth, and nourished by the influx of millions of non-Protestant Americans and the socially disorganizing experience of moving into urban-industrial centers, many older stock Protestants abandoned the orthodoxy of their pre-Civil War childhood. Yet most could not abandon a religious interest, a religious drive, and even, perhaps, a religious temperament that would make secularization into a continuing crisis for their lives.

Ward's life and thought reveal the personal tensions and some of the possible positions a devotee of the new scientific world could encounter as he attempted to integrate the changes in his social reform philosophy with his religious thought. The result of his work was to divorce American democratic faith from its orthodox religious base to a new foundation of naturalistic science. In print, Ward attempted to maintain a detached, disinterested view of religion by claiming that "those engaged in scientific investigation, are for the most part indifferent to religion, and do not feel called upon to devote any time from their pursuits to its consideration."[1] In his personal experience,

135

however, he could never live up to his assertion. On the contrary, deeply influenced by the attraction of religious sentiment, Ward mobilized a considerable amount of his professional writing to combat religious orthodoxy; and, in his last years, he strove to work out a personal reconciliation between his faith in science and his religious temperament.

Ward adopted science as his personal gospel during its early optimistic days when the promise of discovering the ways of nature offered hope for the solving of human problems. The determinism inherent in scientific naturalism, however, soon began to sour that hope as the implications of human responsibility became clearer. Optimism, for some, became a lost cause that was assigned with past mythologies to the junkyard of history. It was from that fate that Ward attempted to salvage a spirit of hope and to rest that spirit in a cosmic faith, ostensibly grounded in science, that could not be shattered as had earlier, prerational religions. The consolation of cosmic science was a monistic reconciliation of the dualisms of mind and matter, soul and body, esthetic awe and naturalistic understanding that linked man with the forces of the universe.

Ward's secularization had its origins, oddly enough, in the strong wave of evangelical Protestant resistance to the influx of Catholicism in the 1850's. The "Know-Nothing" anti-Catholic sentiment directed alike against Irish immigrants, Papal autocracy, and doctrinal errors held sway in the parental Ward home and in the surrounding Illinois villages. Within a decade, Ward would make similar charges against Christendom in general. At some point in his early adolescence, Lester Frank was taken up in a conversion experience, though he himself never mentioned it later, and only a family letter alludes to the early incident.[2]

Ward's diary account of his Pennsylvania coming-of-age suggests that science did not so much subvert his belief, but that theology itself kept him from becoming an adherent of the reigning orthodoxy; for only later was science accepted by him as an alternate faith. His questioning of orthodox theology appears in his earliest diary accounts, but the entries also reveal the depth of his religious interest. It was not unusual for him to attend three or more services on a Sabbath and to find a combined social event and intellectual exercise in the proceedings. "Very interesting," "practical and profound," and "sounded like superstition and disgusted me" were his comments as he evaluated the contents of the weekly sermons.[3]

The intellectual and religious testing came to a peak in the spring of 1861 when one of his teachers attempted to persuade Ward about his duty to God. Ward was supplicated, admonished, and prayed with; he searched himself alone in church and in evening discussions with his fellow students. "My heart was very heavy, and when I sat down in church I could not suppress the tears. I wept and O how my heart felt it! I came home and *tried to pray but I did not know how.*" In his diary, with a penciled in emphasis supplied by Ward fifty years later while preparing his papers for republication, he recorded his discussions about religion with his roommate. "We spoke of it as joined to philosophy and advanced several very curious theories, but my heart *is not yet silent.*"[4] Nor was it to be stilled until late in his lifetime.

Additional diary entries and school papers reveal the unsteady compromise that Ward reached by 1861–1862. In a Friday night debate at the institute over the moral and doctrinal orthodoxy demanded of public school teachers, "a spirit of opposition rose in me," and Ward forced the debators to separate morals from orthodox dogma. In a paper on the coming of the Civil War, Ward had a Southern spokesman defend slavery by citing biblical proofs of its moral position and by attacking Abolitionists, with whom Ward identified, for their irreverence to scripture. Elsewhere Ward was critical of the religious restraints placed on the role of women and on the premarital sexual relations that were causing such ambivalent emotion in his relationship with Lizzie Vought. In a paper on miracles, Ward demonstrated a mildly Unitarian position by quoting Tom Paine, modern science, and "the immutable laws of Nature" to the effect that any belief in contemporary miracles was "stupid." · A Deist "Supreme Power" kept the laws of nature consistent, he contended, although he accepted miracles during the days of the Apostles as the efforts of the "Almighty" to convince an ignorant and unreasonable rabble. But, for the present, he insisted, reliable laws of nature governed the moral as well as the physical world; and any effort to subscribe to a belief in miracles would lead people back into past ages of superstition and would raise up "a sect of disgusting spiritualists."[5]

Evidence is scanty about any religious impact that the Civil War may have had on Ward. Returned to civilian life, he and Lizzie became regular churchgoers in Washington; and they attended various denominations, sects, and even a few Catholic gatherings. By the end of the 1860's, however, the Wards had narrowed their attendance to a Unitarian church that offered a "very good liberal sermon." From the mid-1870's until his departure for Providence in 1906, Ward faithfully paid his monthly pew rent to the same Unitarian assembly. He and Lizzie methodically engaged in Bible reading; but, since they commonly used French and Latin editions, it seems likely that they were interested as much in the language drill as in any religious message. He and his colleagues in the Treasury Department discussed the validity of orthodox doctrines, and the free-thinkers among them loaned Ward works by Voltaire, Spiritualist tracts, and writings of Tom Paine.[6]

In a lyceum debate in 1868, Ward argued that literature, or really the printing press, had performed greater service for civilization than had Christianity.[7] His brief was based more on rationalist argument than on scientific appeals: the historical record of human progress, he charged, demonstrated that men had advanced farther in the four hundred years since the invention of the press than they had in the prior thirteen centuries through Christianity. Why, he asked, had civilization not advanced but actually declined under Christian influence? The answer he proposed was that Christianity had opposed reform in learning, the law, and politics. Only the art of printing that diffused the thoughts of careful thinkers had been able to break the bonds of error and superstition. Predictably, he resurrected the plight of oppressed intellectuals like Galileo, John Bunyan, the Huguenots, and even the witches. Ecclesiastical luxury, he charged, was supported by the starvation of peasants, while church fathers became the most powerful defenders of human slavery. The defense of slavery by the church was his capstone argument; for he suggested that another victim of American slavery had been the credibility of orthodox churches that had equivocated on the issue.

At about this same time, Ward demonstrated his increased anticleric militancy in an angry letter to the *American Presbyterian* in which he denounced its "stupid article" applauding the defeat of John Stuart Mill by the Westminister Constituency.[8] Ward defended Mill as more progressive, humane, and truly religious than any of his cleric opponents. Theological creeds were less important for the good life, he maintained, than the liberty, justice, and education that had absorbed Mill's life. "It matters not under what name, nor by what means its principles are propagated, it is by their fruits that they are known." Socrates, Marcus Aurelius Antoninus, Abraham Lincoln, and Thaddeus Stevens had never subscribed to any orthodox creed, but their actions had revealed them to be "natural Christians."

By the end of the decade, Ward and a half dozen of his more outspoken free thought friends in government offices decided to take the offensive against an orthodoxy in Washington that was applying pressure to deny public halls for free thought meetings. In late November 1869, Ward's living room was the birthplace of the National Liberal Reform League and its publication, *The Iconoclast,* which Ward edited. League members agreed to "unite upon the cardinal principles of hostility to the leading doctrinal teachings of the so-called Catholic and evangelical Protestant Churches, and of zeal for the triumph of reason and science over faith and theology." Their frontal assault on orthodox doctrine and political pressure lasted only a year and a half because of apathy and insufficient funds. While the league lasted, Ward attended at least one free religion convention in Philadelphia and wrote about sixty-five editorials and articles for *The Iconoclast* that analyzed specific doctrines of orthodoxy and reported present and past misdeeds of organized religion.[9] Abraham Lincoln and the historical Jesus received a good press, but other notables were given harsh criticism for blocking progress by appeals to superstitious ideas.

Ward's indignation at the hypocrisy of orthodox religion was brought to the boiling point in the spring of 1870 while he was editing *The Iconoclast.* A roomer of the Wards, one William Marts, a professing evangelical, seduced the Ward's Negro housekeeper, Margaret Woodland, and fled town when his paramour informed him that she was pregnant. When Ward discovered what had happened, he angrily wrote Marts demanding support for the mother and for the mulatto child of his "Christian lust." Ward denounced Marts and the false orthodoxy he symbolized: "You're a fine specimen of a Christian! member of the Y.M.C.A.! always lecturing everybody to get religion! You hypocrite! Religion! Is that religion to seduce your landlord's colored servants and then abscond? Christian! Does Christianity teach you to do such dastardly deeds? Member of the Church! Is this the civilizing influence you were always prating about the church's wielding over its members?"[10] The record is not clear as to whether or not Marts ever paid for his misdeed, but Ward was more convinced than ever that religion and morality were separate human qualities that were confused only by the false apologists of organized superstition.

By the time of the publication of his second book, *The Psychic Factors of Civilization* (1893), Ward was actively engaged in harmonizing his geological and social science research with the institutions of liberal religion in Washington. Throughout the 1890's, Ward lectured to the congregations of the Unitarian All-Souls Church and to the Peoples Church on such edifying topics as "Vegetation of the Ancient World," "The Solution of the Great Social Problems," "Religion from an Anthropological Point of View," "Subjective Psychology," and "The Essential Nature of Religion." Churches, Ward discovered, could be used as lecture halls for popularized science and for the inculcation of ethical behavior based on a rational understanding of nature. Ward's position was not unlike that of Minot Savage, a prominent Boston and New York Unitarian minister, who became a frequent Ward correspondent and houseguest. Savage, like Ward, was a strong evolutionist who had discarded nearly all traditional church doctrine in favor of a continually evolving religion in which beliefs and conscience were viewed as the products of natural evolution. Any divine object of worship was understood as the power of nature operating through the universe.

Quite a circle of evolutionary religionists who corresponded with Ward during the 1890's copiously defined their terms and tried to arrive at common religious meanings of scientific truths. Paul Carus, a Positivist like Ward and the editor of *The Open Court*, a monist religious journal, engaged in long discussions and letters with Ward in which they questioned everything that was subjective and unverified in religious thought. Carus, who visited Ward on several occasions in Washington, found "a difference of terminology between us, but mainly a difference of emphasis upon special aspects."[11] Since truth and nature were one, both Ward and Carus believed, religion had to be based on a scientific investigation of nature and of man's yearnings for religion. Carus had relatively little popular success, a small circulation, and constant disputes with men like Ward who generally believed along similar lines. Unfortunately for their influence, a sectarian spirit among the rationalist religionists was as strong as among orthodox Protestant groups.

Like his friends Carus and Ward, William Torrey Harris, operating from a Hegelian orientation, was also suffering through a profound crisis in religious beliefs. It was amusing, Ward wrote, to point out the ridiculousness of Harris's pompous philosophical profundities that obscured the kernel of scientific fact. Science as the criterion, he claimed, showed Harris's "self-activity" to be the conservation of energy and his Hegelian dialectic as the opposing "radiant" (centrifugal) and "gravitant" (centripetal) forces of physical nature that underlay the biologic evolutionary process.[12]

Ward was a friend also of Thaddeus B. Wakeman, a free thought editor, lecturer, and president of the American Thomas Payne Association. Ward wrote a few brief articles for Wakeman's *The Truth Seeker,* an agnostic newspaper; and he accompanied the publicist to the International Monistic Congress in Germany during the summer of 1911. At Jena, the two visited the spiritual leader of the Monists, Ernst Haeckel, the famed biologist. Wakeman believed with Ward and Haeckel that the only creed that could satisfy modern man was a science that linked man with his natural origins. It was Wakeman who introduced another free spirit, Emily Palmer Cape, to Ward's writings and eventually into his life.

A final member of the same unofficial circle of religious seekers was John Wesley Powell, whose *Truth and Error* was even more unfathomable than the speculative philosophy of Carus and Harris. While Ward counted Major Powell as one of his closest friends and as the major influence upon his life, he risked attack from mutual friends by strongly criticizing Powell's efforts to create a scientific substitute for religion, one Powell called "the Science of Intellectation." As Ward correctly pointed out in a review of the book that embodied the new doctrine, Powell had ended up combatting religious error by slipping into his own metaphysical obscurantism.[13] It had, in fact, been exceedingly difficult for Ward, Powell, Carus, and others to avoid leaping from the scientifically known to speculative constructions dressed in quasi-scientific terminology and mixing unproven scientific analogies with religious beliefs.

To the generation that came of age during the Civil War, it was not enough merely to move away from the doctrinal beliefs of one's evangelical parents. It was personally necessary to argue the moral superiority of a rival value system, one commonly based on the new evolutionary sciences, and to create a logical system of belief that paralleled in form the rejected religion. The psychological influence of traditional beliefs, even in the effort to escape them, continued to be a powerful force in the religious crisis of the age. The peculiar tasks of a generation of scientists devoting much of their lives to the tedious classification of the natural phenomena of their disciplines caused Ward, Powell, and others to slip into thought habits that invented—rather than discovered—hierarchies of categories and that reified abstract classifications into the foundations of new metaphysics. As Ward said of Powell, bricks of a new language were being used to rebuild the same old temple of philosophy.

II   *The Nature Of Religion*

The principal effort in Ward's religious writings was to demonstrate the human origins of religious ideas and institutions and the reactionary character of orthodox beliefs. By the time of his systematic writing in the 1870's, he had borrowed Comte's intellectual framework for viewing human history in three stages of intellectual growth. Like Comte, Ward held that, through gradual evolutionary development from fetishism to monotheism, the more erroneous religious beliefs of the first period of mental life had been weeded out by increased knowledge. Catholicism completed the theological stage of human progress and in turn had had to yield to the second, or metaphysical, stage of rational criticism characterized by Enlightenment figures like Voltaire and Thomas Paine. Much of the early Protestant Reformation was based, Ward contended, on antitheological concepts of intellectual freedom that were spreading over Northwestern Europe. Protestantism, in its turn, however, fell victim of a theological counterattack since the bulk of the European population was not yet able to assimilate the new idea of rationalism. The third stage of scientific Positivism was only now beginning to emerge from the ranks of rationalists.

When men with reason had first tried to solve the problems of nature, Ward theorized, they had developed primitive philosophies or mythologies. Out of mythology grew religion as a product of rational faculties applied to transcendent questions. Religion, therefore, was fundamentally rational, although seldom correct. Its history, in great part, was the history of human thought and as such constituted for Ward essential data for the science of sociology. Ward's interest centered on the biological and psychological origins of religion, relying heavily on the anthropology of non-Western peoples written by Edward Tylor and John Lubbock. The three basic components of religious thought that he analyzed out of the anthropological record were the idea of immortality, belief in spiritual existence, and the existence of a God. Curiously, Ward spent very little time dealing with the third of these concepts; for to him, as to the French astronomer, Pierre Laplace, a "God hypothesis" was unnecessary. The laws of nature had always existed; they were not made to order. Only once in his formal writings did Ward even use the term; on the one occasion, in *Pure Sociology* (1903), "God" was used as a personification of cosmic urge, as the spirit of nature.[14] But the first two conceptions did absorb Ward's interest.

A study of religion by scientific analysis, Ward argued, revealed the natural origins of belief in a spiritual existence and in immortality. Ward adhered to a fully materialistic view of both. "Where matter is not," he wrote, "there is nothing."[15] All early religious ideas were necessarily anthropomorphic, Ward held. Man's fledgling reason interpreted phenomena in terms of the self. The movement of nature suggested that it was alive with intelligence, and from this animated quality of nature emerged fetishism, the earliest form of religion. Out of fetishism, the whole series of beliefs concerning the soul and the spirit grew naturally. Religious evolution followed the general pattern of reducing the number of gods and of giving those that remained greater power. Religion, consequently, was the product of human reason.

The ideas of primitive men, Ward declared, combined both religion and science. To the extent that these concepts were based on awe, fear, and belief, they were religious. But to the extent that they were an effort to explain the unknown, they were gropings for truth and, consequently, the earliest science. Primitive ideas were simply the chaotic stage of thought. It followed from this analysis that religious thought was similarly chaotic, but it was capable of redemption through science. Inseparably entwined with every religion, Ward believed, was a cosmology that tended to develop into a more accurate understanding of the universe—the aim of science. Error yielded to truth, but it did so grudgingly.

All progress in ideas consisted in the gradual elimination of error and in the substitution of truth. All the steps in the evolutionary development of religion had been in this direction, and all heresies were attempts to remove some small part of error from the reigning orthodoxy. Thus Protestantism succeeded Catholicism, and Deism followed Protestantism. Few people were capable of throwing off all error in one fell swoop: "A part must be clung to and cherished a while longer."[16] The progressive character of any age could be judged, Ward held, by the amount of truth found in its philosophy. Truth produced progressive action; error led to regressive action. Progress, therefore, depended upon substituting scientific truths for religious errors. Evangelical Protestants commonly placed the blame for early church scandals on Roman Catholicism, but this view was illogical and unfair, claimed Ward, since most of the infamous actions had occurred before there was any Protestantism. What had been done had been commissioned by Christianity.

The claim of the religious faithful that their belief enhanced morality was sharply criticized by Ward. Morality, he contended, existed independently of religion. Religious appeals to moral sentiment and claims for the responsibility of morality were unfounded; morality and the human desire for it bolstered religion, not the reverse. Primitive morals were based on tradition and public opinion, and such morals were often well defined and persuasive as far as they went. The true influence of religion would have to be measured, said Ward, by the effects of its doctrinal teachings on human conduct. A dispassionate examination showed that the impact of religion had been greatly exaggerated. Looking at those who had abandoned their religious faith, Ward could observe no noticeable change or deterioration in their morality. If there was any change, he reported on the basis of introspection, it was more likely to be in the elevation of moral principle. Rationalism supported morality at least as effectively as religion. Men of scientific background, both believers and nonbelievers, exhibited quite similar morality; no functional difference seemed to be tied to the acceptance of any sectarian creed. It was more often true that criminals and dangerous classes were believers in the prevailing faith and confessed the same when brought upon the scaffold.

While religion served no positive role in promoting human happiness, Ward claimed it did have harmful results. Religion was one of the major parasites on human labor and advancement. All the religious training in history concentrated on one community was useless in solving the basic human problems of want and pain. The amount of energy spent in the futile effort to influence supernatural beings was the withdrawal of energy from the legitimate work of ameliorating man's condition. Attention to the supernatural diverted man from the natural world where the only beneficial changes could be wrought; for, with his eyes concentrated on heaven, man lost sight of the earth. Losses to production resulted also from the withdrawal of priesthoods from the productive arts and of a large proportion of the general population required to support them. Celibacy was also harmful because it attracted the best minds into the clergy and left only the more brutal people to propagate.

More common dangers from established religions sprang from their efforts to protect their privileged position by intellectual censorship and by the manipulation of political power. In

Washington, D. C., for example, Ward attacked the attempt by the Christian orthodoxy to pass "blue laws" that would prohibit the selling of newspapers and the running of streetcars on Sundays. Christian claims to religious preference by such ordinances, Ward reasoned, were an affront to those of other faiths who observed different holy days in the week. Moreover, such restrictions infringed upon the rights of those of other sects who desired the public services in question.[17]

More serious yet, Ward charged, were the various acts of suppression of thought carried on by orthodoxy. Speech and press were commonly controlled whenever the church had sufficient political power to do so. In Spain and Russia, a repressive union of autocratic government and autocratic clergy muzzled the interchange of ideas, suppressed intellectuals, and even banned the sale of his *Dynamic Sociology*. The result for such societies was quite clear, Ward declared: a stagnant society that lacked economic progress and that abounded in mass ignorance and in despotic governments. Religion in alliance with political power meant the suppression of human progress. Any priesthood, if given the opportunity enjoyed in Spain and Russia, would live as a ruling class on the backs of the ignorant masses. Any efforts to promote public education, free public discussion, or uncontrolled scientific work would be suppressed. The sorry religious history of the late-medieval period was visited upon any area that allowed religious orthodoxy to remain in public power.

Ward's unrestrained criticisms of organized religion brought admonitions from friends and fellow progressive reformers about Ward's need to moderate his position if he wished to gain a larger hearing from the public. Richard T. Ely, a reform economist and Christian layman interested in the utilization of the social sciences by the Social Gospel movement, gently chided Ward that he failed "to distinguish between the real nature of Christianity and the abuses of the church." Albion Small, a former minister who, like William Graham Sumner, had left the church for sociology, also attempted to convince Ward that his religious position was exaggerated and that he underestimated the changes that had occurred among liberal churchmen. A few Unitarian ministers also criticized Ward in more open terms for beating dead carcasses, and they insisted that Ward's "new ethics" of social improvement were already being preached from many pulpits in the country. "You are not a very regular attendant on any intelligent and cultivated minister," wrote one critical pastor, "or you could not have been lead [sic] into the mistake of stating that what you call the old ethics holds way in the church...."[18] Undoubtedly, Ward continued to find pleasure in posturing against the excesses of the evangelism of his childhood and adolescence; and, although he most likely assigned a greater static quality to American Protestantism than in fact existed, the proponents of the "old ethics" he attacked were still a majority of American churchmen.

III   *The Conflict Between Religion And Science*

During the Gilded Age, the literature of both religion and science recognized the scientific world view as an enemy of organized religion. Scientific spokesmen, led by such formidable penmen as Edward L. Youmans, editor of *Popular Science Monthly*; John William Draper, whose early version of the confrontation in his *History of the Conflict Between Religion and Science* (1875) set the stage; and Andrew Dickson White in *A History of the Warfare of Science with Theology in Christendom* (1896), all adopted a battlefield analogy to describe what seemed for them an irrepressible conflict. *Popular Science Monthly* was one of the first periodicals to which Ward subscribed, and Youmans had been instrumental in publishing *Dynamic Sociology*. Draper's book was read by Ward when it first appeared, and he was corresponding with White at Cornell University before his book appeared.

People on both sides of the issue felt a crusading commitment for their cause. The rejection of traditional religion by a number of men of science became a religion in its own right, leading to what a later historian of the conflict calls "dogmatic scientism."[19] For most of the scientific contestants, including Ward, the conflict was viewed as natural and inevitable; it was not viewed as the product of belligerent partisans; it was considered the nature of science to advance while religion could only take the defensive protecting an outdated epistomology and cosmology.

Ward, by choice and by early inclination, joined the battle. As editor of *The Iconoclast*, Ward's editorials and articles in 1870 and 1871 reiterated the basic conflict between religion and rationalism, even before the battle in his mind had assumed the additional character of a Darwinian struggle for survival. The efforts of organized religion to insinuate itself into the Constitution, to prevent the introduction of science into the common schools and colleges of the land, and to subvert freedom of opinion by fettering free speech and the press were the issues that *The Iconoclast* promised to combat. And so it did for a year and a half by reviewing rationalist books, denouncing particular religious and government acts of suppression, and poking satirical fun at the more outrageous behavior of pompous church divines.

In a farewell editorial in *The Iconoclast*, Ward announced a shift in strategy from an open confrontation with error to a new "Hope."[20] The new strategy that Ward announced to remove error was to move more quietly, but more profoundly, by propounding scientific truths incompatible with religious ones. Likening the growth of intellectual liberty to the renewal of a diseased plant, Ward noted that new growth gently pushed up from beneath, supplanting the blighted outer leaves that gradually withered and disappeared. Planning for a long campaign, Ward foresaw scientific truths as growing up within the camp of religious believers that in several generations would supplant "Genesis" with "Geology." A gradual reconstruction of ideas would be more positive, he argued, than negative frontal assaults that only antagonized the public and strengthened its opposition. Liberals should not be discouraged, he advised, for mental liberty was "an irresistible tide" that had produced over the past three centuries a mighty progress.

Twenty years later when Albion Small, his sociological collaborator, pleaded with Ward not to antagonize potential readers by his revived attacks on religion, Ward responded belligerently, "I do not write for the feeble minded." Despite Ward's revised strategy, he felt no inclination to compromise his views to suit the sensitivities of the superstitious. Ward was especially pleased with the burning of *Dynamic Sociology* by Russian censors in the 1890's because of its tendency to sap belief in God by its materialistic and atheistic spirit.[21] Autocratic priest-ridden Russia was an appropriate enemy to acquire, and the act of suppression validated Ward's thesis about the power of free, scientifically derived ideas to liberate captive people.

Even scientific Washington, D. C., was not immune to counterattacks from organized orthodoxy. In 1894, Samuel P. Langley, the director of the Smithsonian, expunged from the Smithsonian *Report* for 1892 an article by Ward and another by WJ McGee, fellow freethinker in the Geological Survey, for fear that they might cause political trouble for the Smithsonian because of their antireligious content. After the articles had been printed and bound, Langley grew apprehensive of public and congressional reaction during the current economic depression and so had the pages deleted from the published report. The affair was a local sensation in Washington where most of the press— and, somewhat embarrassingly for Ward, many of the churches— came to his defense, or rather to the defense of freedom of speech and press. Langley had certainly overreacted; Ward's and McGee's thesis that the mind and the soul were the product of physical evolution was nothing new to any who were at all acquainted with their work. Yet Langley was quite correct in arguing that the conclusions were speculative, were not based on empirical evidence gathered during their geological research, and were suggestive that scientists were being paid to write speculative metaphysics. The local Anthropological Society immediately published the addresses in special editions; and Ward, not unmoved by the publicity, accepted the episode philosophically as what one might expect because of the political power of the orthodox.[22]

At any rate, there was no denying that a conflict existed. For Ward, the conflict between the two institutions was not just over ideas but also over the practices and ethics that had become associated with the two bodies of thought. Attending a meeting of Felix Adler's Ethical Culture Association, Ward expressed great admiration for "the new ethics" based on science for the relief of suffering and the promotion of human welfare.[23] This hopeful sign of the times, he believed, was another expression of applied sociology and signalled the emergence of ethics geared to a pleasure economy, ethics that would be dynamic rather than static in maximizing human liberty and happiness.

The conflict between religion and science, Ward believed, stemmed from their common origin in the minds of early men. Originally the two had been fundamentally identical in that they were rational efforts to explain phenomena. Those conclusions that relied on supernatural explanations and on the spiritual content of nature combined to establish religion on a basis of error; explanations based on a natural interpretation of phenomena constituted science and progressively brought nature under man's control. The supernatural had always given way to the natural since the real was more powerful than the false, and it had been on this advancing line that the warfare of science and religion had been waged for centuries. Religion had always exhibited deep hostility to the advancement of knowledge, Ward contended, because knowledge threatened to explain away the necessity for supernatural powers and for the priesthood that found a comfortable livelihood in manipulating the symbols of erroneous belief.

As knowledge, science, and intelligence spread slowly among men, the strong religious spirit retreated. Some scientists, Ward pointed out, believed that the rapid advances of science would completely remove religious authority when all aspects of man and nature had naturalistic explanations. Within the historic period, the territory once belonging to the gods had been seized by astronomy, physics, chemistry, and geology. That of biology had only recently been almost fully brought under the province of science, while the present battlefield, Ward noted, was over the area of moral and social phenomena. There was now even a rational and naturalistic explanation of religion itself with his own analysis revealing its origin and content as a natural development.

Religion had always been distrustful of change since the status quo was viewed as the natural, normative condition created by spiritual beings. Any artificial change, therefore, was an attempt on the part of man to thwart the will of the gods. The pattern was true throughout history. A prime example, relished by Ward, was the storming and burning of the library at Alexandria in 391 A.D. by fanatical Christians. The flicker of light from the

Classical world was extinguished by religion. Centuries were required for a new development of learning to rise up. When it did, religion fought back with the persecution of Copernicus and Galileo, the martyrdom of Bruno and Servetus, and a systematic warfare upon science and material civilization.

The greater part of the evils from which humanity suffered, Ward affirmed, was really due to error—to the false conclusions drawn from inadequate premises. Religion supported error and, consequently, was responsible for much of man's troubles. Error was a function of religion and was consequently a force for inappropriate morals—bad morals—that was not encountered by those who followed science as a basis for truth. In fact, a chronology of religious customs was a list of human misery: human sacrifice, self-mutilation, asceticism, superstition, zoolatry, and witchcraft. Heresy and the persecution of those accused were more recent offenses that were made possible only in more civilized societies where advanced knowledge and education developed independent minds capable of doubting old errors and of arriving at new interpretations of phenomena. The opposition had always been dogmatic—no amount of demonstration of new knowledge had made much difference. "Those who believe things because they are impossible are not going to believe anything because it is proved," observed Ward.[24]

Truth was a powerful weapon in man's arsenal for combatting the hostile forces of the environment. Quoting Robert Ingersoll, Ward noted that one sure way to improve the universe would be to make health catching instead of disease. But, just as it was the mission of medical science to replace disease with good health, so was it the mission of all science to do away with error by replacing it with truth. The logic of the matter did not allow him, or any other scientist, to stand outside the contest; it compelled him to take the offensive against religion. Either frontal or rear attacks could be mustered either by attacking the false premises of religion, as did Ingersoll, or by promoting truths that were incompatible with error, the tack Ward followed. But in either case it was necessary to act since the mission of science was to remove error. The march was irresistible; religion had constantly lost from the first "and must continue to lose to the last."[25]

IV *Spiritualism*

Spiritualism had a curious fascination for Americans in the late nineteenth century; and the interest shown by some scientists in psychic and occult behavior and in exceedingly nonconformist religious conceptions of immortality compatible with their scientific beliefs was not surprising since the hazy boundaries between where science might profitably explore new phenomena and where neurotics and charlatans cavorted had not yet been determined. As Unitarian Minot Savage cautioned Ward, men of science could not write off such investigations as those of William James since even hypnotism was once claimed as fraudulent. Spiritualists published a serious, scientifically oriented journal, the *Religio-Philosophical Journal,* after the Civil War; and respected scientists of the caliber of Simon Newcomb, Samuel Langley, and G. Stanley Hall formed the American Society for Psychical Research. Nor were Spiritualists only proponents of an extraworldly existence; quite a number, like Robert Dale Owen, Benjamin Orange Flower, and Victoria Woodhull, were active reformers who managed to unite their social and religious dissidence. Even the American Association of Spiritualists entered into humanitarian and constitutional reform questions.[26]

Ward, too, had not been unaffected by the Spiritualists' confrontation with the various orthodoxies. He had never ruled Spiritualism completely out of question during his early attacks on religion, but he was always skeptical. He had subscribed to the *Religio-Philosophical Journal* in his Washington clerkship days, and he had unsuccessfully tried to publish in its columns. During the 1860's in particular, but also throughout his life, he was interested in attending Spiritualist demonstrations, although usually to criticize their lack of scientific method. In an early article in *The Iconoclast* on "the new faith," he reported that the current interest in Spiritualism showed that other present religions were moribund and that people were searching for a new life.[27] People who were intent on living forever, as the old church taught, but who could not accept the illogical doctrines that permeated orthodoxy, rushed into another system short on doctrine but long on hope for immortality. As for himself, Ward declared, he hoped the world could be spared another reign of religion before intellectual and moral improvement finally absorbed all human devotion. Elsewhere in *The Iconoclast*, he directed attention to various Spiritualist and occult happenings that confounded orthodox authority and that appeared to be based upon little understood principles of nature that science had not yet explained.

Spiritualism, for Ward, was one of a number of radical religious alternatives worthy of consideration; in addition, it offered an opportunity to discover a naturalistic basis for religious belief. Because his scientific curiosity was aroused by psychic investigations, he and Lizzie attended seances and even had their heads examined by a phrenologist. While he was sympathetic, if amused, by the tales of the Spiritualists he met in the ebullient free religion movement, Ward acknowledged that it was possible that there might be scientific validity to certain types of Spiritualist powers. As of yet, however, science had not objectively verified them; and most, he believed, were surely fraudulent. Trances, however, had been common to mankind from its earliest days, he wrote; and visions could be voluntarily produced by practice and by fasting. Not all seers, prophets, and faith healers were "frauds" in any literal sense since cultural acceptance and the power of the mind to convince itself explained the deep faith of the true believers.

Yet, after all his experience with Spiritualists, it seemed "very strange," Ward remarked, that those who propounded countergravitational forces of levitation and other supranatural feats could not demonstrate them by the strict laws of physical experimentation. On the contrary, the conditions that were viewed as conducive to the Spiritualists' claims were those of darkness, mystery, and concealment—the very antithesis of those laboratory conditions that had been proved effective in the systematic discovery of reliable truths. Both the British and American societies for psychical research, he complained, failed to recognize the frequency of coincidences and wasted their time hunting for ghosts, none of which had yet been found. The world of even reputable scientists still clung to error, he sighed.[28]

The more deeply Ward became involved in his own paleontological work in the 1880's and the more developed his own

scientific world view became, the less open he was to the
Spiritualist's challenge to orthodox science. By the 1890's, Ward
was aghast by even having his name associated with Spiritualism.
An incident that provoked his anger was his appointment to
the advisory council of the Congress on Psychical Science
affiliated with the 1893 Chicago Columbian Exposition. Having
previously accepted a position on the Geology Council of the
exposition, he angrily wrote to the editor of the *Religio-
Philosophical Journal* that he had assumed that a similar invitation to sponsor a psychical science congress was equally scientific
for "there was no subject in which I was more interested than
psychical science."[29] But, when he discovered that the congress
was a front group for Spiritualists and Theosophists, he was
horrified; and he demanded a retraction in the journal that
would indicate that his name would never be used in "religious
propagandism." The Spiritualists, he protested, were attempting
to drag the name of science into their service, just as orthodoxy
had repeatedly appealed to authority to bolster its position. It
was a fraud, Ward charged, to confuse the public by sponsoring
Spiritualists' doctrines of telepathy, clairvoyance, and spiritual
afterlife in Chicago papers together with legitimate scientific
topics like hypnotism, hallucinations, and psychometry. The
congress, he predicted, would be taken over by "the zealots,
fanatics, and paranoiacs of the land, who will convert it into
a pretty Pandemonium." He had no objection to being called
an "orthodox agnostic," if the congress wished to damn him;
but he did take exception to being called a "materialist" by
Spiritualists when he had tried to show repeatedly that mind
and intellect were "wholly *immaterial*" functions of the brain
and when the Spiritualists themselves were investigating very
material spirits in table tippings, raps, and physical apparitions.

   In a follow-up letter, Ward also explained his fear of being
swallowed up in the Spiritualist quicksand.[30] Established scientists like the Englishmen Alfred Russell Wallace and William
Cookes, he wrote, had strong enough scientific accomplishments
to protect their reputations even when they dabbled in the
occult. But for others, like himself, who were less secure of their
record, "even the libellous charge of looking that way ... ruins
him for any useful purpose as everybody thenceforth looks

askance at him." Psychical science was fine, but Spiritualism was only for the religious cranks among whom Ward did not number himself. An orthodox and respectable religion of science had developed, and Ward worshipped in its laboratory temple.

V *Immortality*

The possibility of spiritual phenomenon existing in the empirical world available to science left open at least a slender hope for immortality. For people undergoing secularization, the most difficult belief to jettison was that of continued existence, at whatever level, after physical death. Consequently, since the issue of immortality was one of the most critical debates in American religious life of the late nineteenth century, it accounts to a substantial degree for the interest in Spiritualism and in other sectarian movements. The debate was tied to developments in evolutionary science that found no empirical basis for any immortal essence; thought and feeling appeared to be solely a function of the nervous system with no separate existence. Yet the desire to maintain life or some form of consciousness after the inescapable fact of death was a powerful force for scientists, as well as for laymen, to combat.

The question of immortality engaged Ward repeatedly during the development of his religion of science. In his last years, he accepted several ideas on immortality which, while neither religious in the sense of any of the reigning religious systems nor particularly capable of providing emotional comfort for the masses, did at least satisfy his requirement of rationality and relieved his restless heart which continued to raise the immortality question long after he had discarded any notions of universal deities. In essence, the mature Ward accepted in place of traditional Christian belief his assurance about the continuance of one's ideas and deeds after death and about the indestructibility of all atoms out of which evolved future life and history.

Ward knew from experience that a belief in immortality was a strong weapon in the orthodox defense; as a doubting youth, he himself had wondered about his and Lizzie's chances. In the formal writings of middle life, Ward took the position that a belief in traditional immortality held back the lower classes more than any other of the false ideas of religious sects. Always haunted and oppressed by fears like savage peoples, they suffered from the priesthood's threats of eternal damnation that promised pains for eternity beyond the very real ones of the present. "This diabolical doctrine," Ward charged, "has been the cause of more suffering than all other religious errors combined, but it has been the main dependence in keeping the masses under complete spiritual subjection."[31]

As with all religious beliefs, Ward attempted to explain man's drive for immortality on natural principles. The original source of the idea, he held, was found in the early functioning of man's reason as he attempted to understand certain types of phenomena outside his small storehouse of reliable information. The free play of mind on personal subjective awareness and on the objective mysteries of nature led people in nearly all societies to reach similar views about the reality of spirit and about its continuation after death in an immortal state. Consequently, the preservation of spirit through immortality was intimately involved in the origins of religion; and the belief was strengthened by the "priestcraft's" eventual manipulations of men through appeals and threats to the future life of the consciousness.

Contemplating future bliss conceivably created real pleasure, but it was more than counterbalanced, Ward reasoned, by the fear that resulted from the idea of eternal suffering. But regardless, given the difficulty of drawing up a moral balance sheet, any influence that a belief in immortality had on morality was one of a static nature, not a dynamic one. If such a belief made men happier, wrote Ward, it did nothing to make them wiser or more energetic in changing society. Instead, its influence was to dampen men's ardor for the conquest of physical nature by which alone all true progress was accomplished. Furthermore, Ward argued, immortality concepts were nonprogressive because they belittled the importance of the present state of material life and because they worked to withdraw mind and muscle from productive labor into useless contemplation of that which was not real and never could become so. Some apologists argued that a belief in immortality offered a solace for abused mankind but Ward maintained that true progress resulted from an increase in actual enjoyment, not imaginary expectations.

"Those whose only pleasure consists in hope, or anticipation, really have no enjoyment," he warned; and those who attempted to find cause for belief in the cautious public positions of most scientists equally deluded themselves.[32]

The failure of the great moral systems of the past to improve existing conditions of society had led, Ward suggested, to their gradual transformation in more modern times into religious systems. Since the promises for this life were dropped when it was found that they could not be fulfilled, religious hopes were placed upon a subsequent future life in which the failure of fulfillment could never be proved. As the failure of promises for this life led to those of a second, so in Ward's own age, he believed, the claims of future life were coming more and more into question. There had been a rapid and increasing amount of dissatisfaction as people demanded better things in this life. Both moral and religious systems had failed to deliver the goods they had preached. Science was rapidly moving into the vacuum and could already show results.

In response to a questionnaire by a religious newspaper, Ward initiated a series of dogmatic articles about immortality that completely rejected any orthodox understanding of the subject and that left in its stead a form of scientific Quietism. In his essays Ward contended that immortality in the form of continued consciousness after death could not occur. Personal consciousness, he said, was the result of molecular activity in the brain. When the brain ceased functioning, so did the possibility of mental existence. The effects of drugs, poisons, and injuries to the brain all showed, he maintained, that consciousness and memory could not be separated from the physical organs that created and maintained them. The inability of man to recall states of consciousness or events antecedent to his present existence also supported his view that "mind" or "soul" began and ended with physical life. Any belief to the contrary was not only outside the pale of science but belonged to "mythology and magic." But then startling his orthodox readers in the *Christian Register* with a deft change of pace, Ward announced that his conception of consciousness did not mean that science was skeptical about the immortality of the soul. Indeed not! Based on a true knowledge and appreciation of natural laws, "science postulates the immortality, not of the human soul alone but of the soul of the least atom of matter. Consciousness results from the eternal activities of the universe, is their highest and grandest product, and not one atom nor one atomic movement is ever lost. The immortality of science is the eternity of matter and its motions...."[33]

Only the truly philosophical could find personal reassurance and spiritual strength from this cold analysis from the heights of a cosmic worldview. Nonetheless, Ward found humorous satisfaction in the large number of querulous communications that arrived in response to this materialistic interpretation of immortality. Writing the next month in Paul Carus's *The Open Court*, Ward expanded on his statement of belief.[34] Science—as the new gospel—had posited an infinite existence within the elements of nature. The material elements of the universe had always existed, Ward affirmed, and their activities were perpetual and as inseparable from the elements as human consciousness was from the unique material organization of the brain. All phenomena were made of these particles, constantly changing in organized form over eons of time. All the powers of man were but the force of nature intensified many thousandfold through organization; neither the total amount nor the motion of the universe had been increased. There existed, had always existed, and would ever exist the indestructible and unchangeable elements and powers "out of which through similar processes, equal and perhaps far superior, results may be accomplished. This is the immortality that science teaches, the faith that inspires the genuine student of nature, and this pure and ennobling sense of truth he would scorn to barter for the selfish and illusory hope of an eternity of personal existence."[35]

As Ward approached his seventies and the end of his years, he did not falter from the logic of his scientific faith; but neither could he renounce his ego. Since the coldly rational comfort of contemplating the future of his immortal elements was insufficient, Ward channelled much of his remaining thought and energy into another form of immortality that other rationalists, like his friend, Paul Carus, had suggested. Instead of acts of piety or an introspective examination of his conscience, Ward after 1907 placed increasing importance and, at the end, his nearly total effort into compiling a collection of all his non-scientific published papers with autobiographical comment and into commissioning Emily Palmer Cape, a kindred spirit, to write his biography. One's works and ideas would remain more immortal after death, he calculated, if they were broadly available on the printed page.

VI *A Partial Reconciliation*

In Ward's reflections in his late sixties about Herbert Spencer that applied to himself, Ward wrote that old men never adopted religious doctrines that they had rejected earlier in their careers.[36] Rather, growing wiser in understanding the history of mankind, they began to realize the "devious paths" that humanity had been compelled to follow in its slow evolution toward modern civilization. Unaware of the natural origins of man and society and systematically deprived of such information in their youth, men required a lifetime of scientific study to understand the true history of the human race and the paradox that error in particular circumstances could be of utility. The historical utility of certain errors that Ward was now willing to admit belonged to the field of religion. He had not really relaxed his criticism of organized Christianity, but he had begun to accept the sociological institution of religion as the fulfillment of basic human needs and as potentially useful in any future "socio-cratic" state.[37]

In finding a legitimate role for religion in the future, Ward looked back into the early history of man. The emergence of religion he found in the "natural" development of a group safety ethic among primitive men. The religious institution had developed among rational men as a protective mechanism in the near absence of instincts that protected the subrational world. In order to preserve life, nature had put a premium on the development of feeling to move organisms to gain pleasure and to repel pain. Feeling motivated plastic organisms to perform acts that would preserve their existence. There was no "design" at work in any anthropomorphic sense; nature moved by independent fortuitous action. The nerve focus for feelings centralized in spinal cords and eventually in the brains. Working by indirection, the brains guided the feelings into longer life and greater reproduction. The larger the brain, generally, the greater the ability to soothe feelings and to promote the interests of the living organism. Meanwhile, the surplus mental powers of the animal with the most sophisticated brain—man—moved out into other areas of activity related only indirectly to the basic functions of protecting the life and continuation of the species. Animals with less complex brains built up inherited reflex actions—instincts—that provided them with basic protection since their mental processes alone were insufficient for preservation. Man had few such instincts, for his natural selection had not required them. Instead, his brain had produced ideas which, transmitted by language over the generations, had created basic social institutions that provided much the same sort of automatic protection that instincts provided animals.

One of the early problems that the brain and its mental activity posed for man, left unsolved by inherited instincts, was the unlimited range of desires encouraged by thought. The drive to maximize pleasure, for example, led to dangerous practices—to practices of lust and adventure that endangered not only the life of the individual but the preservation of the species. That same mind, however, in formulating conceptions of the self and the surrounding environment, created notions of spirits and eventually anthropomorphic deities that curbed the unlimited impulses promoted by the brain. Since primitive moral codes could not be made self-enforcing based on reason alone, it was necessary to call in power far stronger than either law or conscience in the form of a super spirit with eternal rewards and punishments; and thus emerged the vengeance of the gods to terrify men into the preservation of social order. Dimly and intuitively perceiving the dangers of desires no longer proportional to life functions, early man, through the joint action of natural selection and reason, produced religion to curb the excesses to which his powerful ego would have otherwise led. This religious tendency, Ward suggested might even be called "religious instinct."[38]

The fear and awe of man, who realized the majesty of a power outside himself, made him receptive to religious ideas. Natural environmental power was viewed as supernatural since early man was unable to understand the rational organization of natural forces; and man's objective was to gain a right relationship to that power in order to protect self and group. The primary purpose of religion from the very beginning, then, had been salvation. Just as early myths were invented to deter people from economic self-seeking at the expense of the group, so now sermons in orthodox churches operated as a conservative economic force. Similarly, the powerful reproductive passions were restrained by religion to deter promiscuity that otherwise would have led to neglected offsprings and would have posed a consequent threat to the continuity of the species.

Religion surely guarded order, Ward acknowledged, but it did not strive for progress. It restrained will rather than attempting to direct it by reason for new human advantage. Progressive agents of feeling sought to employ and strengthen man's capacity for enjoyment; but religion, fearful of its excesses sought to limit enjoyment. In a biological analogy, Ward likened religion to heredity and reason to variation. The former preserved the type, but the latter modified it. It was not progress that either heredity or religion opposed, but change; and progress in both the organic and social realms, operating in a natural dialectic, was a compromise between centripetal and centrifugal forces. Both forces were legitimate and necessary, he admitted, especially during the earliest days when reason and its products, like the economy they created, were marked by scarcity. But now, as abundance in the production of both material comforts and reliable knowledge was available, or shortly would be, man would necessarily have to change both his economic and his religious thought. From a life of scarcity and pain—with institutions based on such facts of life—man now had to reconstruct his ideas and his social organization to a new order of abundance and pleasure. The old religion of fear and restraint that had once served a valuable function would need to be retired, and it would have to be replaced by a new scientific orientation to life that prepared man to inherit this world, not the next. A secular millenium was at hand.

Early religion had yielded to the demands of reason whenever they were safe for man, though abnormal historical growths of religious asceticism, self-abnegation, and "puritanism" now threatened to obscure the valuable functions religion had once served. As soon as rational guarantees were furnished that new ideas and practices were useful and valuable, religion should yield to them. Nonetheless, an inevitable question remained: "Shall science, brushing aside one after another the cobwebs that obscure the vaults of nature, at last so completely lay bare her secrets that no hidden terrors will remain? . . . Will science finally swallow up religion, assume its functions, and stand wholly in its stead?"[39]

To answer the question, Ward equivocated. Rather than the strong affirmative that he had voiced to the question earlier in life, he now in his last years admitted a way out for religion. If the natural role of religion were accepted as its essence, as he had explained it, then religion would not necessarily have to be abandoned; rather, it could preserve a place for itself by placing all confidence in reason and by ceasing to obstruct the realization of the noblest capabilities of man's nature. Given the recognized resistance of people to change old values embodied in earlier institutions, Ward was willing to allow the old religious forms to continue if they were replaced by a new scientific content. In this fashion church buildings would become halls of science, sermons would be scientific lectures, and the revered scriptures would be the more profound generalizations drawn from the mass of new reliable information about man and nature that had been discovered through the various scientific disciplines.

Interestingly enough, several liberal ministers in orthodox denominations shared Ward's religious concerns and sent him church programs showing the incorporation of his articles on meliorism, the relationship of the sexes, and progress into their sermons. " 'Broadening the Way to Success,' " wrote one minister, "is a much better sermon than I can ever preach. . . ." This interest in his writings, limited as it was, gave Ward some hope that the infiltration of his ideas was beginning to leaven the quality of the message in more advanced congregations. Religion, he told the congregation of the liberal Peoples Church in Washington, was currently going through the larval stage of development; soon it would become adult "with wings."[40] Wings were always fluttering in the background for Ward and other scientific freethinkers.

In his last years at Brown University, Ward repeatedly expressed the idea that man needed a religion to express his inner feelings and thoughts. He even talked about writing a short volume about the topic to show that a scientist might hold a religious faith if it were based on scientific teachings rather than on illusory revelations. Scientific thought in its highest meaning, he held, was not cold and materialistic; the deeper the comprehension of nature's laws, the more noble, grand, and free were the expressions of human relationships. Recognition of the continuity in nature as the evolution of all things could unite humanity instead of dividing it as contemporary religions did. Recognition of continuity, furthermore, made people appreciate that no one was ever fully independent since each inherited body, soul, and idea came from those who had gone before. Realization of this principle, the old worker believed, inspired a person to add to the whole that those who followed would inherit. Love of nature created a connective link between the moral and the esthetic in life. Since nature was infinite, man's contemplation of it would bring the mind into contact with the infinite.

Ward brought this decidedly moderated interpretation of religion into the classroom with him. To a freethinker friend who had criticized Ward for going soft on religion before students, the old iconoclast replied, "You say I am conservative in my lectures to my classes. Of course I must be. But I find no difficulty in it. I put such interpretations on all the old things that they do not conflict with the truths of science." In discussing the evolution of ideas and institutions, Ward pointed out the parallels between religious scriptures and scientific findings. As he explained to his students, earlier people had personified the evolutionary process by creating mythological exploits to account for the natural world. The great flood was a geographical history of the earth as the land rose out of the sea; the Garden of Eden was the region where the human race originated; and the dispersal of Noah's sons symbolized the peopling of the earth. In fact, the book of Genesis was "the ontogenetic recapitulation of the phylogenetic evolution of the universe." With this approach, Ward found little criticism from his orthodox students; they were "specially pleased" with his judgment that religion would not pass away or be merged into ethics. Instead, he preached, "It has a grand mission of its own; *As it began in awe and fear of nature, it will end in awe and love of nature.*"[41]

Ward brooded about how to incorporate these feelings into a form acceptable and attractive to thinking people. At four o'clock in the morning, while visiting Hamburg, Germany, he noted in a letter to a friend that he had risen from bed to draw up a title and thesis for a book. The revealing title he set down, "Monism the True Quietism, or the Continuity of Nature the only Faith that can satisfy the emancipated Soul," accurately reflected the scientific Quietism that his contemplation of nature was leading to. Spiritual peace, he proposed, could be found by accepting a cosmos without beginning or end—one in which individual men died but mankind lived. By reflecting on the reality of "continuity" in nature, this scientific Quietism allowed a person to forget himself and to become conscious of the immortality of the processes of nature. At sea on his last trip to Europe in 1911, he wrote that "the immensity of space, the tremendous waves, and the sublime starry heavens impress me with a sense of cosmic unity that fills me with life and infinite joy."[42] The heart that would not be still in its youth and in its middle years had found a refuge in nature that violated neither Ward's emotional longings nor his scientific rationalism.

CHAPTER 7

"The Possibilities of Conscious Effort": An Appraisal

LESTER Ward once remarked that his life was "plain and unvarnished" and contained "nothing of any very remarkable interest." His own contribution in writing and ideas, he acknowledged with unaccustomed modesty, was "simply a product of the *Zeitgeist*" of the second half of the nineteenth century.[1] On one level of thought, Ward was quite accurate in his estimate, as a mid-twentieth-century critic sought to prove empirically by tallying the limited citations to Ward's work in paleobotanic and sociologic scholarship after his death.[2] Yet the number of index citations to Ward in later natural science or social science works seems hardly to exhaust the possibilities of either his significance or his interest to students of American life and letters.

Ironically, Ward's constraint in evaluating the importance of his life prefaced a proposed twelve volume collection of his *lesser* writings with autobiographical comment! The breadth of interest and the quantity of writing revealed in this undertaking, as well as in his major works, suggests that Ward deserves careful, if critical, attention as a late-nineteenth-century social commentator. While Ward is unknown to the public and to most scholars in the twentieth century, he has been considered an important interpreter and formulator of democratic ideals by such discerning historians of the course of American thought as Charles Beard, Ralph Henry Gabriel, and Henry Steele Commager.[3] This present study of Ward has sought in a similar context to examine the areas in which Ward attempted to rekindle democratic aspirations and the particular social applications of scientific ideas that he brought to bear on American life.

165

Ward's reputation as an American thinker has undoubtedly suffered because of his writing skills. At worst, his works were verbose; his prose, abstruse; his vocabulary, pretentious; and his style, oratorical. To the extent that this was true, the responsibility rests with his desire to prove himself as learned as were Comte and Spencer—his models for intellectual attainment in content and style—and with his formative student experience in self-expression as a debater and orator seeking the attention that his social breeding did not warrant. A self-made writer suffered defects as noticeable as those in the personality of self-made men. The lack of a sense of humor in Ward's case, not surprisingly, is found in both his character and in his writing. Similarly, his difficulty in bearing lightly his moderate success from low beginnings—after immense effort—marred his writing by the frequent prominence of his ego. Too often Ward translated into cosmic law his own experience and fancies of the passing moment, and in later life he questioned the personal motives of any who criticized his sociology.

Another problem in Ward's writing style stemmed from his dual occupational handicaps of being both a government bureaucrat and a natural scientist. The heaviness of expression found among both groups lay just below the surface in Ward and was only reinforced by his entry into the social science field so heavily influenced by pedantic German scholarship. Given these factors relative to his writing, the only surprise is that Ward wrote with as clear and forceful a style as he did.

His popular articles and his writings attacking laissez-faire and other schools of thought that he believed harmful to society are generally structured quite logically and are presented in clear, expository fashion. After the reader has either grasped the meaning of—or ignores—the score or so of Greek-derived terms that Ward commonly used, his writing becomes reasonably rewarding. While the quality of academic writings in sociology may be a low standard of comparison, Ward's sociological works, particularly his articles in the *Journal of American Sociology* and in *Pure Sociology* and *Applied Sociology,* read as well, if not better, than contemporary works in the field. And for those interested in lucid summaries of the various sciences, vintage 1880's, *Dynamic Sociology* is excellent. It was only when Ward moved into philosophical speculation, as he did in his longer works and in his articles for metaphysical journals, that his abstractions and his problems with logical consistency legitimately distress readers.

But Ward's significance for American intellectual life was not dependent upon his literary skills or upon the accuracy of his predictions regarding the future evolution of American society. As the preceding chapters have attempted to demonstrate, Ward's importance rests upon his efforts to reconcile early-nineteenth-century democratic values and assumptions with the socio-intellectual changes of his own day. In particular, Ward was concerned with establishing a social theory that would be consistent both with the new truths being established in the natural sciences—led by evolutionary theory in biology—and with the hopes for personal advancement and happiness that constituted the inner dynamics of the American democratic dream. The gulf between the dream and the reality of American experience formed the creative tension within which Ward lived and thought. By strength of will, he attempted in his life to achieve the American dream intellectually as well as socio-economically. By the end of his years, he even began to see himself as the symbol of his beliefs in democratic social theory.[4]

Resisting the powerful and often contrary views of Manchesterian laissez-faire economic theory, evangelical Christian determinism, and newer theories of human determinism generated by the natural sciences, Ward sought to fashion a theory and a society—grounded on reason and experience—that would create open-ended possibilities for humanity. Nourished on democratic and religious idealism and weaned on traumatic economic and social change, Ward considered all social phenomena to be susceptible to men equipped with the right ideas and with the confidence necessary to sustain their labors. As he explored the origins and nature of the major social institutions concerned with education, government, economics, sexual relations, and religion, Ward attempted to justify not present practice, but a realistic hope for all people—regardless of race, sex, or class position—to achieve greater happiness. Ward affirmed life: economic well-being, intellectual understanding, heterosexual sexuality, and awe in the presence of the creative forces of the universe. He attacked on sight those men, theories, and institutions that denied these possibilities for all humanity; and he later sought scientific support to justify his position.

It was the speculative indifference of philosophy and science to the problems in American life—ideological as well as physical—that most threatened American society, Ward believed; and it was his effort to bridge the chasm between intellect and reform. Public opinion drifted, he feared, while "philosophy and science stand back on the old platform of laissez-faire and leave the field to an army of social reconstructionists with their conflicting and bewildering panaceas." Few indeed, he found, were the efforts "to bring a recognition of law and sound scientific principles to bear upon the problem." Because of the seriousness of political drift, the open clashes with mounting antagonism between labor and capital, wasted lives in the cities and on the farms, and the growing chasm between the educated with opportunity and the ignorant without, the only alternative for scientists with democratic values was "to help on a certain evolution by averting an otherwise equally certain revolution."[5]

The function of democratic intellectuals, Ward maintained, was to influence the conduct of men by instilling progressive principles in their minds and by undermining fatalistic principles that frustrated their will and their ability to shape environment creatively. Positive social theory demanded and suggested the means for achieving "the satisfaction of all natural wants, material and spiritual, the means of rearing a family free from all fear of want, of educating children to the limit of their capacities and tastes, of building attractive homes stocked with all enlightening agencies, of moving about in the world sufficiently to shake off all narrow provincialism, and of living in the great stream of human progress."[6]

With this constellation of reform assumptions and specific social objectives, Ward helped to keep alive in a new social setting the unique combination of Enlightenment and Romantic values that had coalesced in America by the early nineteenth century. The task of adapting and implementing those values in the face of vastly different social conditions and shattering intellectual discoveries was formidable; with no foreordained outcome, the responsibility rested with each generation. A few among the intellectual leaders of the progressive reform movement in the early 1900's recognized Ward's role in keeping the dream alive during the late nineteenth century by harnessing it to the authority of evolutionary science—as would the Beards in the 1930's, Gabriel in 1940, and Commager in the 1950's and 1960's. Frederic C. Howe, an independent Progressive leader in New York and Cleveland—and a later bridge himself to the reform activities of Franklin D. Roosevelt's New Deal administration—was one of these; and in 1912 he wrote the seventy-year-old professor at Brown University

to tell you how great a debt I owe to you for the things you have written. And when I express my own intellectual obligations I feel that I am expressing the obligations of a nation for the new interpretations you have given to life, to society, to the place of men and women, to the whole social awakening which has been finding expression during the past ten or fifteen years. . . . You took the heritage which I received from the old school of thought and gave it a new organizing central thought that has been as it were a core about which other things all arranged themselves. And I think you have done that for all of us, whether we are able to trace the parenthood of our thoughts or not. Certainly the whole social philosophy of the present day is a formative expression of what you have said to be true.[7]

While Ward held no monopoly on progressive assumptions or on efforts to establish an intellectually respectable reform rationale, his analysis constituted one of the few indigenous intellectual efforts to create a science of society that was consistent with traditional democratic social and political values. His social philosophy never lost sight of the possibilities of conscious effort: "It is a reaction against the philosophy of despair that has come to dominate even the most enlightened scientific thought. It aims to point out a remedy for the general paralysis that is creeping over the world, and which a too narrow conception of the law of cosmic evolution serves rather to increase than to diminish. It proclaims the efficacy of effort, provided it is guided by intelligence. It would remove the embargo laid upon human activity by a false interpretation of scientific determinism, and without having recourse to the equally false conception of a power to will, it insists upon the power to act."[8] For generations yet to come, ones beset by similar malaise of spirit and intellect, Lester Ward's life and social philosophy held open the possibilities of a future in which humanity possessed the capacity to improve the conditions of its existence.

Notes and References

Chapter One

1. *Glimpses of the Cosmos*, 6 vols. (New York, 1913–1918), I, lxvi.
2. Quoted in Emily Palmer Cape, *Lester Frank Ward: A Personal Sketch* (New York, 1922), p. 21.
3. *Glimpses of the Cosmos*, I, lxviii.
4. St. Charles *Argus*, March 1858, cited in *Glimpses of the Cosmos*, I, 24–32.
5. Cape, pp. 24–25.
6. *Young Ward's Diary*, edited by Bernhard J. Stern (New York, 1935), *passim*.
7. *Ibid.*, p. 69.
8. Quoted in Cape, p. 61.
9. *Young Ward's Diary*, p. 107.
10. "The Reciprocal Obligations of Parents and Children," *Childhood*, I (December 1892), 9–11.
11. *Ibid.*, p. 10.
12. Quoted in Ward's pension file, National Archives, Washington, D. C.
13. Quoted in Cape, p. 64.
14. *Young Ward's Diary*, p. 133.
15. *Ibid.*, p. 162.
16. *Ibid.*, p. 171.
17. *Young Ward's Diary*, p. 202.
18. "Washington City" (Manuscript, 1869, Ward Collection, Brown University).
19. *Ibid.*, p. 2.
20. Quoted in a Ward letter to Edward Young, May 6, 1876. Ward personnel file and service letters, National Personnel Records Center, St. Louis.
21. *Glimpses of the Cosmos*, III, 204.
22 Quoted by Stern in *Young Ward's Diary*, p. 318.
23. *Young Ward's Diary*, p. 319.
24. Ward personnel file and service letters.
25. Quoted in Cape, p. 127.

26. *Applied Sociology* (Boston, 1906), p. 276.

27. *Glimpses of the Cosmos*, III, 202.

28. *Ibid.*, p. 204.

29. Ward to Welling, June 9, 1887, Ward letters, Brown University.

30. "Review of *What Social Classes Owe to Each Other*," *Man*, IV (March 1, 1884), 1 and 4. His *Forum* articles include "Broadening the Way to Success," II (November 1886), 340–50; "The Use and Abuse of Wealth," II (February 1887), 549–58; "False Notions of Government," III (June 1887), 364–72; "What Shall the Public Schools Teach?" V (July 1888), 574–83; "Our Better Halves," VI (November 1888), 266–75; "Causes of Belief in Immortality," VIII (September 1889), 98–107; and "Genius and Women's Intuition," IX (June 1890), 401–408.

31. *The Psychic Factors of Civilization* (Boston, 1893).

32. *Outlines of Sociology* (New York, 1898).

33. *Glimpses of the Cosmos*, VI, 218.

34. *Pure Sociology* (New York, 1903).

35. *Applied Sociology.*

36. *A Text-Book of Sociology* (New York, 1905).

37. H. Heath Bawden, "Review of *Pure Sociology*," *American Journal of Sociology*, IX (November 1903), 408–15.

38. *Glimpses of the Cosmos*, VI, 206.

39. Samuel Chiles Mitchell, "Some Recollections of Lester F. Ward and James Q. Dealey," *Social Forces*, XVI (October 1937), 45.

40. *Ibid.*

41. Miscellaneous newspaper file, Ward Collection, Brown University.

42. James Q. Dealey, "Masters of Social Sciences: Lester Frank Ward," *Social Forces*, IV (December 1925), 260. Mrs. Cape's remark is written in pencil in the loose files of the Ward Collection.

Chapter Two

1. *Applied Sociology*, p. 106.

2. *Young Ward's Diary*, pp. 212–15.

3. *Ibid.*, p. 68.

4. "The Age of Steel" (Manuscript, dated 1866–1867, in the Ward Collection, Brown University), p. 1.

5. *Ibid.*, p. 207.

6. "Broadening the Way to Success," pp. 340–50; *Glimpses of the Cosmos*, IV, 34.

7. "Broadening the Way to Success," p. 343.

8. *Young Ward's Diary*, pp. 278, 318.

9. Laurence Cremin, *The Transformation of the Schools: Progressivism in American Education* (New York, 1961), pp. viii–ix.

10. "Education" (Manuscript, 1871–1873, Ward Collection, Brown University), p. 311.

11. *Pure Sociology*, p. 573

12. *Ibid.*

13. *Applied Sociology*, p. 220.

14. "Early Education and Precocity," *Childhood*, II (November 1893), 394.

15. *Dynamic Sociology*, II, 500.

16. *Glimpses of the Cosmos*, IV, 267–68.

17. *Applied Sociology*, p. 311.

18. "The Struggle of Today," *The Truth Seeker* (New York), February 17, 1912; and *Pure Sociology*, p. 195.

19. *Report on the Petrified Forests of Arizona* (Washington, D. C.: Government Printing Office, 1900).

20. Mrs. John F. Ottley, "Outside Educational Forces Department," *The North Western Monthly*, VIII (December 1897), 333–35.

21. "Education that Educates" (Manuscript, January 8, 1912, Ward Collection, Brown University).

22. George Sims to Ward, September 1909. Ward letters, Brown University.

23. "Education and Progress," *Plebs Magazine* (Oxford), I (December 1909), 244.

24. Edward A. Ross, *Social Control* (New York: Macmillan, 1901).

25. William Harris, "Reviews," *Educational Review*, VI (January 1893), 84.

26. John Dewey, "Review of *The Psychic Factors of Civilization*," *Psychological Review*, I (July 1894), 400–408.

27. Edward L. Thorndike, "Education: A Sociologist's Theory," *Bookman*, XXIV (November 1906), 290–94.

28. Cremin, p. 98. Also see Rush Welter, *Popular Education and Democratic Thought in America* (New York: Columbia University Press, 1962), pp. 230–37.

Chapter Three

1. John C. Burnham, "Lester Frank Ward as Natural Scientist," *American Quarterly*, VI (Fall 1954), 259–65; and Arthur Hollick, "Lester Frank Ward," *Science*, XXXVIII (July 18, 1913), 75–77.

2. Hollick, pp. 75–77.

3. *Outlines of Sociology*, p. 210.

4. "Haeckel's Genesis of Man," *Penn Monthly,* VIII (April-July 1877), 266–84, 348–67, 528–48.

5. "Cosmic and Organic Evolution," *Popular Science Monthly,* XI (October 1877), 672–82.

6. *Glimpses of the Cosmos,* IV, 95.

7. "The Local Distribution of Plants and the Theory of Adaptation," *Popular Science Monthly,* IX (October 1876), 676–84.

8. *Dynamic Sociology,* II, 44–73.

9. "Mars and Its Lesson," *Brown Alumni Monthly,* VII (March 1907), 159–65.

10. See the discussion by George W. Stocking, "Lamarckianism in American Social Science, 1890–1915," in *Race, Culture, and Evolution* (New York, 1968), pp. 234–69.

11. "Neo-Darwinism and Neo-Lamarckism," *Proceedings,* Biological Society of Washington, D. C., VI (1891), 11–71.

12. Stocking, p. 256.

13. "Fortuitous Variation," *Nature,* XL (July 25, 1889), 310.

14. "Neo-Darwinism and Neo-Lamarckism," p. 54.

15. *Ibid.,* pp. 63–65; and "The Transmission of Culture," *Forum,* II (May 1891), 312–19.

16. "Neo-Darwinism and Neo-Lamarckism," p. 65.

17. "The Transmission of Culture." The misleading title was supplied by the editor and not by Ward who complained of the terminology. *Glimpses of the Cosmos,* IV, 243–45.

18. "The Transmission of Culture," pp. 314, 319.

19. "Weismann's New Essays," *Public Opinion,* XIII (September 10, 1892), 559; "Review of Weismann's Theory of Heredity," *Public Opinion,* XVI (October 5, 1893), 11–12; and "Weismann's Concessions," *Popular Science Monthly,* XLV (June 1894), 175–84.

20. *Pure Sociology,* pp. 214–15, 311, 499, 573.

21. *Applied Sociology,* pp. 120–22.

22. Charles B. Davenport, *Heredity in Relation to Genetics* (New York: American Eugenics Association, 1911), p. 1.

23. Mark H. Haller, *Eugenics: Hereditarian Attitudes in American Thought* (New Brunswick, N.J.: Rutgers University Press, 1963), *passim.*

24. "Broadening the Way to Success," pp. 340–45.

25. "Review of *An Outline of the Theory of Organic Evolution* by Maynard M. Metcalf," *American Anthropologist,* VII (March 1905), 118. See also his "Review of *The Problem of Age, Growth, and Death* by Charles S. Minot," *American Anthropologist,* X (December 1908), 668–69.

26. *Applied Sociology,* pp. 113–242.

27. "What Brings Out Genius," *Washington Star*, December 22, 1907, pt. 3, pp. 11, 14.

28. *Ibid.*, p. 11.

29. "Eugenics, Euthenics, and Eudemics," *American Journal of Sociology*, XVIII (May 1913), pp. 737–54.

30. *Ibid.*, p. 754.

31. *Ibid.*, p. 740.

32. *Ibid.*, p. 741.

33. *Ibid.*, pp. 753–54.

Chapter Four

1. Cyrenus Ward, *A Labor Catechism of Political Economy* (New York: By the Author, 1878).

2. Cyrenus Ward, *The Ancient Lowly: History of the Ancient Working People* (Washington, D. C.: By the Author, 1889).

3. Cyrenus Ward, *The Ancient Lowly: The Origins of Socialism* (Washington, D. C.: By the Author, 1900).

4. Henry O. Ward to Lester Ward, September 18, 1892, Ward letters, Brown University.

5. Miscellaneous newspaper file, Ward Collection, Brown University.

6. *Young Ward's Diary*, pp. 14–66.

7. See Jules Cohn, "The Political Philosophy of Lester Frank Ward" (Ph.D. dissertation, Rutgers University, 1958); and Henry Steele Commager, "Introduction" in *Lester Ward and the Welfare State* (Indianapolis, 1967), pp. xi–xxxviii.

8. *Applied Sociology*, p. 128.

9. *Dynamic Sociology*, I, 69–70.

10. *Applied Sociology*, pp. 338–39.

11. *Dynamic Sociology*, I, vii.

12. See Richard Hofstadter, *Social Darwinism in American Thought*, rev. ed. (Boston, 1955).

13. *The Psychic Factors of Civilization*, pp. 245, 258–66.

14. *Ibid.*, p. 320.

15. *Ibid.*, p. 286.

16. *Pure Sociology*, p. 20.

17. "The Enlargement of State Functions" (Manuscript, dated 1886–1887, Ward Collection, Brown University).

18. *Outlines of Sociology*, p. 276.

19. *The Psychic Factors of Civilization*, p. 323.

20. *Dynamic Sociology*, II, 243–44.

21. *Ibid.*, I, 40–41.

22. *The Psychic Factors of Civilization*, p. 309; *Dynamic Sociology*, I, 37, 227.

23. *Outlines of Sociology*, p. 36.

24. *Pure Sociology*, pp. 319–20.

25. *The Psychic Factors of Civilization*, p. 327.

26. *Outlines of Sociology*, p. 291.

27. See Ward letters and miscellaneous papers, Ward Collection, Brown University.

28. Jones to Ward, June 24, 1910, and September 16, 1910, Ward letters, Brown University.

29. Minassian to Ward, September 24, 1909, Ward letters, Brown University.

30. *Glimpses of the Cosmos*, VI, 233.

31. "Sunrise Club Dinner," *New York Sun*, December 28, 1909, p. 6.

32. James Fleming, "The Role of Government in a Free Society: The Conception of Lester Frank Ward," *Social Forces*, XXIV (March 1946), 257–66; and Conway Zirkle, *Evolution, Marxian Biology, and the Social Scene* (Philadelphia: University of Pennsylvania Press, 1959), pp. 169–71.

33. *Applied Sociology*, p. 11.

34. *Ibid.*, p. 10.

35. *Dynamic Sociology*, II, 597.

36. "Title to the Soil" (Manuscript, 1871, Ward Collection, Brown University).

37. *Applied Sociology*, pp. 93–94; "False Notions of Government," *Forum*, III (June 1887), 372.

38. See the letter files of the Geological Survey, National Archives, Washington, D.C.; and Ward's personnel file, National Personnel Records Center, St. Louis.

39. *The Psychic Factors of Civilization*, p. 324.

40. *Dynamic Sociology*, II, 573–80.

41. "The Sociological Position of Protection and Free Trade," *American Anthropologist*, II (October 1889), 289–99.

42. "Little Cause for Fear: Prof. Ward's Opinion About Coxey's Movement," *The Washington News*, April 23, 1894, p. 3.

43. *The Psychic Factors of Civilization*, p. 329.

44. Ward to White, July 26, 1896, Andrew White papers, Cornell University.

45. *Ibid.*

46. *Pure Sociology*, p. 49.

47. Editor to Ward, November 19, 1896, Ward letters, Brown University.

Chapter Five

1. *Glimpses of the Cosmos,* III, 172.
2. *Glimpses of the Cosmos,* III, 177.
3. Dealey, pp. 257–72; Harry Elmer Barnes, "Lester Frank Ward," in *An Introduction to the History of Sociology* (Chicago, 1948), pp. 173–90; Don Martindale, "Lester Ward," *The Nature and Types of Sociological Theory* (Boston: Houghton-Mifflin, 1960), 69–72.
4. *Pure Sociology,* p. 15.
5. *Ibid.,* pp. 145–47; *Outlines of Sociology,* p. viii.
6. William Graham Sumner, *What Social Classes Owe to Each Other* (New York: Macmillan, 1883).
7. The classic study is Hofstadter's *Social Darwinism in American Thought.*
8. "Review of *What Social Classes Owe to Each Other*" in *Glimpses of the Cosmos,* III, 301–305.
9. "Competition as a Basis of Economic Theory," *Annual of the American Economic Association* (Washington, D. C., 1895), pp. 84–85.
10. "Herbert Spencer's Sociology," *The Independent,* LVI (March 31, 1904), 730–34.
11. "Mind as a Social Factor," *Mind,* IX (October 1884), 569.
12. *Glimpses of the Cosmos,* VI, 268.
13. *Ibid.,* 269–71; "Social and Biological Struggles," *American Journal of Sociology,* XIII (November 1907), 289–99.
14. Lester Ward, "Social Darwinism," *American Journal of Sociology,* XII (March 1907), 709–10.
15. *Applied Sociology,* p. 110.
16. "Education" (Undated manuscript, Ward Collection, p. 292, Brown University).
17. *Young Ward's Diary,* pp. 54–58, 105.
18. *Ibid.,* pp. 178, 180, 192, 230–31, 286, 305.
19. *Ibid.,* pp. 262–64.
20. Ward to White, July 26, 1896, White Collection, Cornell University.
21. *Dynamic Sociology,* I, 477–78, 541; Ward to White, July 26, 1896, White Collection, Cornell University.
22. *Pure Sociology,* pp. 206–11.
23. *Ibid.,* pp. 213–15.
24. Ludwig Gumplowicz, "An Austrian Appreciation of Lester F. Ward," *American Journal of Sociology,* X (March 1905), 648–51.
25. "Evolution of Social Structure," *American Journal of Sociology,*

X (March 1905), 589–605; letter from Ward to Mrs. Cape, September 27, 1910, quoted in Cape, p. 95.

26. Lucy Moten to Ward, January 1, 1896, Ward letters, Brown University.

27. G. F. Cook to Ward, February 7, 1896, George M. Lightfoot to Ward, November 30, 1896, Beulah Morgan to Ward, August 15, 1898, George Washington Ellis to Ward, February 25, 1909, Ward letters, Brown University; and Jervis Anderson, "Profiles: A. Philip Randolph," *New Yorker*, XLVIII (December 2, 1972), 86.

28. W. H. Burnett to Ward, January 14, 1911, Ward letters, Brown University.

29. See Charles Hunt Page, "Lester Frank Ward," in *Class and American Sociology: From Ward to Ross* (New York, 1940), pp. 29–69.

30. *Pure Sociology*, pp. 201–15; and "Social Classes in the Light of Modern Sociological Theory," *American Journal of Sociology*, XIII (March 1908), 617–27.

31. *The Psychic Factors of Civilization*, pp. 162–68; see also "A Review of *The Theory of the Leisure Class*," by Thorstein Veblen, *American Journal of Sociology*, V (May 1900), 829–37.

32. *Applied Sociology*, pp. 100–101, 307–308; and *Dynamic Sociology*, II, 249–50.

33. *Pure Sociology*, p. x.

34. This literature is sympathetically presented by John C. Burnham in *Lester Frank Ward in American Thought* (Washington, D. C., 1956) and attacked by Robert C. Whittemore, "The Contemporary Relevance of Lester Ward," *Southern Journal of Philosophy*, I (Winter 1963), 27–39.

35. See Simon Patten, "The Failure of Biologic Sociology," *Annals of the American Academy*, IV (May 1894), 919–47.

36. Ward letters, Brown University, *passim*. Some of this correspondence has been edited by Bernhard J. Stern and is cited in the bibliography.

37. Albion Small, "Lester Frank Ward," *American Journal of Sociology*, XIX (July 1913), 78.

38. Clipping from the *Washington Post*, December 29, 1905, no page enumeration, Miscellaneous newspaper file, Ward Collection, Brown University.

39. Albion Small, "Points of Agreement Among Sociologists," *Publications of the American Sociological Society*, I (March 1907), 55–71.

Chapter Six

1. *Dynamic Sociology*, I, 693.

2. *Glimpses of the Cosmos*, I, 24–32; letter from Lorenzo Ward to Lester Ward, January 20, 1884; letter from Sarah Prince to Ward, August 29, 1909, Ward letters, Brown University.

3. *Young Ward's Diary*, p. 87.

4. *Ibid.*, pp. 50–51.

5. *Ibid.*, pp. 54–55, 109. "The Day of Miracles is Over" (Manuscript, 1861–1862, Ward papers, Brown University).

6. *Young Ward's Diary*, pp. 219–39.

7. *Ibid.*, pp. 251–53.

8. *Ibid.*, pp. 274–76.

9. *Ibid.*, pp. 308–14.

10. Ward to William G. Marts, May 23, 1870, Ward letters, Brown University.

11. Carus to Ward, August 9, 1891, and December 5, 1894, Ward letters, Brown University.

12. *Glimpses of the Cosmos*, V, 142–49.

13. "Review of *Truth and Error* by J. W. Powell," *Science*, IX (January-February 1899), 126–37, 259–63.

14. *Pure Sociology*, p. 136.

15. "The Natural Storage of Energy," *The Monist*, V (January 1895), 247–63.

16. *Applied Sociology*, pp. 51–63, 82.

17. "To the Editor," *Daily Morning Chronicle* (Washington, D. C.), October 30, 1871, p. 2.

18. Oliver Dean to Ward, July 8, 1896. See also Richard T. Ely to Ward, July 30, 1890; Small to Ward, September 18, 1890, and March 28, 1894. Ward letters, Brown University.

19. Paul A. Carter, *The Spiritual Crisis of the Gilded Age* (DeKalb, 1971), p. 15.

20. "Hope," *The Iconoclast*, II (April 1871), 1.

21. Kennan to Ward, July 15, 1891; Theodore Sigel to Ward, September 30, 1896, Ward letters, Brown University.

22. "Status of the Mind Problem," *Special Papers*, Anthropological Society of Washington, I (1894), 1–18.

23. *Applied Sociology*, p. 28.

24. *Ibid.*, p. 76.

25. *Dynamic Sociology*, II, 269, 305.

26. Carter, pp. 87–107.

27. "The New Faith," *The Iconoclast*, I (November 1870), 1.

28. "The Natural Storage of Energy," *The Monist*, V (January 1895), 247–63.

29. Ward to editor of the *Religio-Philosophical Journal*, March 13, 1893, Ward letters, Brown University.

30. Ward to Eliot Coues, March 21, 1893, Ward letters, Brown University.

31. *Applied Sociology*, p. 94.

32. *Dynamic Sociology*, II, 284.

33. "Lester F. Ward," *The Christian Register* (Boston), April 7, 1887, p. 211.

34. "The Immortality that Science Teaches," *The Open Court*, I (May 26, 1887), 199–201.

35. *Ibid.*, p. 201.

36. "The Value of Error," *The Rationalist Press Association Annual and Ethical Review* (London, 1909), p. 8.

37. *Applied Sociology*, pp. 64–65.

38. "The Essential Nature of Religion," *International Journal of Ethics*, VIII (January 1898), 169–92.

39. *Ibid.*, p. 190.

40. Rev. J. O. Stevenson to Ward, February 18, 1896. See also Aaron Beebe to Ward, November 1, 1898; Rev. Bradford Leavitt to Ward, January 28, 1898; and "The Solution of the Great Social Problem" (Address delivered to the Peoples Church, October 22, 1893), Ward letters and papers, Brown University.

41. Ward to Emily Palmer Cape, November 7, 1910, quoted in Cape, pp. 109-10.

42. *Ibid.*, p. 50.

Chapter Seven

1. *Glimpses of the Cosmos*, I, lxxviii; "Preface" to the second edition, *Dynamic Sociology*, 2 vols. (New York, 1896), I, vii.

2. Burnham, *Lester Frank Ward in American Thought*.

3. Charles A. Beard, "Lester Frank Ward," *New Republic*, CI (November 15, 1939), 119; Charles A. and Mary R. Beard, *The American Spirit* (New York: Macmillan, 1942), pp. 405–12; Ralph H. Gabriel, *The Course of American Democratic Thought* (New York: Knopf, 1940), pp. 204–209; and Henry Steele Commager, *The Amercian Mind* (New Haven: Yale University Press, 1950), pp. 204–16, and *Lester Ward and the Welfare State*.

4. *Glimpses of the Cosmos*, I, xiii–xiv.

5. "The Utilitarian Character of Dynamic Sociology," *American Anthropologist*, V (April 1892), 97–103.

6. *Applied Sociology*, p. 329.

7. Howe to Ward, July 27, 1912, Ward letters, Brown University.

8. *Applied Sociology*, p. iii.

Selected Bibliography

PRIMARY SOURCES

1. *Manuscript Materials*

Ward Collection in the John Hay Memorial Library of Brown University is the major depository of Ward materials, including a collection of his scrapbooks, letters, and unpublished manuscripts.

National Archives in Washington, D. C., has Ward's letters and reports to the Geological Survey along with his military records and pension file.

National Personnel Records Center in St. Louis holds Ward's personnel file and service letters.

Library of Congress Manuscript Division contains Ward's book manuscripts.

Andrew D. White Collection at Cornell University holds Ward letters not found in the Ward Collection at Brown University.

2. *Published Letters and Diary*

STERN, BERNHARD J. ed. "Giddings, Ward, and Small: An Interchange of Letters." *Social Forces*, X (March 1932), 305–18.

——————. "The Letters of Albion W. Small to Lester F. Ward. *Social Forces*, XII (December 1933), 163–73; XIII (March 1935), 323–40; XV (December 1936), 174–86; XV (March 1937), 305–27.

——————. "Letters of Alfred Russell Wallace to Lester F. Ward." *Scientific Monthly*, XL (April 1935), 375–79.

——————. "The Ward-Ross Correspondence, 1891–1896." *American Sociological Review*, III (March 1938), 362–401.

——————. *Young Ward's Diary*. New York: Putnam's, 1935. This diary from about 1860 to 1871 is extremely useful.

3. *Articles* (listed chronologically)

"The New Faith." *The Iconoclast*, I (November 1870), 1.

"The Local Distribution of Plants and the Theory of Adaptation." *Popular Science Monthly*, IX (October 1876), 673–83.

183

"Haeckel's Genesis of Man." *The Penn Monthly,* VIII (April-July, 1877), 266–84, 348–67, and 528–48.

"Cosmic and Organic Evolution." *Popular Science Monthly,* XI (October 1877), 672–82.

"Politico-Social Functions." *The Penn Monthly,* XII (May 1881), 321–36.

"Darwin as a Biologist." *Proceedings,* Biological Society of Washington, D. C., I (1882), 81–86.

"Scientific Basis of Positive Political Economy." *International Review,* XII (April 1882), 352–65.

"Remarks on Spencerian Social Darwinism." *Transactions,* Anthropological Society, II (1882), 31–33.

"Review of *What Social Classes Owe to Each Other.*" *Man,* IV (March 1, 1884), 1–4.

"Mind as a Social Factor." *Mind,* IX (October 1884), 563–73.

"Moral and Material Progress Contrasted." *Transactions,* Anthropological Society, III (1885), 121–36.

"Broadening the Way to Success." *Forum,* II (November 1886), 340–50.

"The Use and Abuse of Wealth." *Forum,* II (February 1887), 549–58.

"Lester F. Ward." *The Christian Register* (April 7, 1887), p. 211.

"The Immortality That Science Teaches." *The Open Court,* I (May 26, 1887), 199–201.

"False Notions of Government." *Forum,* III (June 1887), 364–72.

"What Shall the Public Schools Teach?" *Forum,* V (July 1888), 574–83.

"True and False Civil Service Reform." *Historical American,* I (July 1888), 25–30.

"Our Better Halves." *Forum,* VI (November 1888), 266–75.

"Some Social and Economic Paradoxes." *American Anthropologist,* II (April 1889), 119-32.

"Fortuitous Variation." *Nature,* XI (July 25, 1889), 310.

"Causes of Belief in Immortality." *Forum,* VIII (September, 1889), 98–107.

"The Sociological Position of Protection and Free Trade." *American Anthropologist,* II (October 1889), 289–99.

"Genius and Women's Intuition." *Forum,* IX (June 1890), 401–408.

"The Course of Biologic Evolution." *Proceedings,* Biological Society of Washington, D. C., V (1890), 23–55.

"The Transmission of Culture." *Forum,* XI (May 1891), 312–19.

"Neo-Darwinism and Neo-Lamarckism." *Proceedings,* Biological Society of Washington, D. C., VI (1891), 11–71.